Ole Goes to War

Men from Norway Who Fought in America's Civil War

1880 regimental reunion
of the Wisconsin 15th

Ole Goes to War
Men from Norway Who Fought in America's Civil War

is a companion volume to Vesterheim's exhibition

Norwegians in the Civil War
February 22 – September 1, 2003

Ole Goes to War

Men from Norway Who Fought in America's Civil War

Jerry Rosholt

To Hoot.
Jerry Rosholt
Christmas 2003

Vesterheim Norwegian-American Museum
Decorah, Iowa

This volume was funded through a gift from the

GOVERNMENT OF NORWAY
to honor the
125th Anniversary of
Vesterheim Norwegian-American Museum

Cover photo: *Henry Steen,* Steen Collection, Vesterheim Norwegian-American Museum archive.

Book design by Zelda Productions, Decorah, Iowa

Table of Contents

Acknowledgments

Several people shared their own research and expertise with this project, and deserve my thanks:

Scott Cantwell Meeker, Middleton, Wisconsin, has thoroughly researched the Wisconsin 15th and posted the regimental roster and history on the internet.

Robert Larsen, Oregon, Wisconsin, searches for soldiers in all Wisconsin regiments and shared his findings.

Bruce Larson, Minneapolis, Minnesota, provided records of Norwegian soldiers in Minnesota units.

Dee Grimsrud, an archivist at the State Historical Society of Wisconsin, Madison, both located and provided data on many individuals in Wisconsin units.

I am also indebted to Gene Estensen, Marietta, Georgia and Faust Gertz, Decorah, Iowa, for guidance in putting my data on the Internet.

Dirk Rosholt, New York, New York, offered technical advice on how to handle the research material and diligently corrected spelling, punctuation, and typing errors.

I owe much thanks to Vesterheim's staff: to executive director, Janet Blohm Pultz, for encouraging me, and to curator Tova Brandt, media director Charlie Langton, and office manager, Katie Lawless, for help in editing and assembling the text.

And thanks to the hundreds of people who have sent me stories and photocopies of the military records of their ancestors.

– Jerry Rosholt

Preface

Back in 1941, writing in his book, *Norwegians in New York 1825-1925*, A.N. Rygg noted with regret that it "would be highly interesting if by any means it could be determined how many Norwegians took part in the Civil War as soldiers or sailors, but it is altogether too late to attempt a check-up now."

Rygg hadn't counted on Jerry Rosholt.

Jerry graduated from Luther College in 1948, and worked in the Twin Cities during the 1950s, writing radio news shows for Cedric Adams among other things.

Then Jerry left the Midwest to spend more than a quarter century at NBC News, chasing stories over four continents, writing for Chet Huntley and John Chancellor, and working as field producer for NBC's coverage of the India-Pakistan War, the U.S.-U.S.S.R. Strategic Arms Limitation Talks (SALT), the Sadat–Begin peace talks, several Civil Rights demonstrations, Vietnam War protests, and national political conventions from 1964 to 1986.

Jerry likes to say that, when he retired, he "faded into the New Jersey Pine Barrens." But in 1997 Vesterheim curator Darrell Henning coaxed him out again. At Darrell's urging, Jerry returned to Decorah, his old college town, and went to work searching for Norwegians in America's wars. He keeps finding them – more than A.N. Rygg or anyone else ever expected – and has uncovered fascinating stories about many of them in the process.

This book, the exhibit it accompanies, and most of all the extensive database of Norwegians in the Civil War now available on Vesterheim's website, exist only because Jerry consented to bring his reporter's sense of accuracy and his talent for storytelling to bear on one of the pivotal moments in American – and Norwegian-American – history. It is an ongoing project, one he began and continues as a volunteer.

Historians, genealogists, Civil War buffs, and most of all, Vesterheim, are forever in his debt.

– Janet Blohm Pultz, Vesterheim Executive Director

Introduction

When the Wisconsin 15th Regiment, the 'Norwegian Regiment,' marched from their training grounds to their first battles in 1862, the Nora Society of Chicago presented them with a banner. The banner featured a blue field in the corner and red and white horizontal stripes, just like the flag of the United States. Instead of stars, the blue field held the lion of Norway next to the American eagle and the motto, "For Gud og Vort Land!" (For God and Our Country). The banner's symbols and motto perfectly illustrate the combination of Norwegian identity and American patriotism that inspired many Norwegian immigrants to take part in the American Civil War. Many, but not all.

Why would an immigrant come to the United States knowing it was on the brink of war? What motivated Norwegian men to enlist? Did all Norwegian immigrants react to the war in the same way? The stories, letters, photos, and histories contained in this book offer some answers to those questions.

This book is a companion to the exhibit *Norwegians in the Civil War* and contains a sampling of the 10,000 Civil War records on Vesterheim's website. The entire project is the product of six years of research, thousands of miles of travel, dozens of public presentations on the topic, and many generations of families preserving the stories and experiences of their ancestors. The one person responsible for bringing all of those elements together is Jerry Rosholt. Jerry is the author of this volume, guest historian for the exhibit, popular speaker for groups across the country, and researcher of over 10,000 entries in the complete database of Norwegian-born soldiers and sailors who became involved in the pivotal conflict of American history. His work has been an invaluable contribution to Vesterheim's mission of preserving the heritage of Norwegian immigrants to America.

Because the database listings will eventually include all Norwegians in all American wars, as information turned up on a Norwegian enrolled in another war, he was included in this study. Similarly, when records indicated a soldier or sailor was born in Sweden or Denmark, he was included in the database. The vast majority of listings, however, are the 6,500 Norwegian men with ties to specific Civil War military units. In addition, there are 3,500 names that have not been linked to specific units, and are probably duplicates of the 6,500. The past 140 years have generated many books and articles about Civil War soldiers, not all with the amount of detail necessary to match duplicate listings. Also, many families may know a great-grandfather's civilian name, but never knew he enlisted with a different name.

This project is ongoing. As more people search the database and compare Vesterheim's information with their own family records, more duplicates will be matched, and more history will be accurately preserved for future generations. Vesterheim will continue to support the ongoing study of Norwegian experience in the Civil War and in all other periods of American history.

– Tova Brandt, Vesterheim Curator

Thrond and Ingeborg Steen and their sons who fought in the Civil War:
Martin, Charlie, John, Henry and Otto (Theodore not pictured)

Those Steen Boys

Charles Steen got to the recruiting line early the morning after President Lincoln's first call for troops to save the Union. Charlie was one of 53 Norwegians to become soldiers in Minnesota's First Regiment of Infantry Volunteers.

He was also one of six brothers born in Norway who enlisted in infantry regiments. He and his brothers all became corporals or sergeants, all fought in major battles, four became prisoners of war, and all came home.

They were the sons of Thrond and Ingeborg Steen, who in 1853 immigrated with their boys, then ages 7 through 19, to a farm in Glenwood Township, east of Decorah, Iowa. Charlie was 25 when Lincoln's call came, working in St. Paul for Minnesota governor Alexander Ramsey.

The Minnesota First, with its 53 Norwegians, fought through many battles: Bull Run, Antietam, Chancellorsville, Spotsylvania. Charlie, it is said, was always out front. He became a corporal, then sergeant, and finally his company's first sergeant.

Then came Gettysburg.

On the second day of that epic struggle, the First was behind a low stone wall that runs the length of Cemetery Ridge. The Minnesotans were shooting at lines of Confederate soldiers coming toward them, relentlessly firing as they came marching across a wheat field and up a hillside, seeming not to be affected by the bullets and minie balls raining down on them from the Northern regiments lining the ridge.

Behind the Minnesotans, Union reinforcements were also coming, galloping toward the ridge, hurrying to help.

General Winfield Hancock, close behind the Northern lines, was standing beside his horse, watching the fighting, seeing the Southerners coming on, getting ever closer, already within steps of the low stone wall. Turning, he could

Sergeant Charles A. Steen, Minnesota 1st Infantry, Company A

see behind him the fresh Union troops, now running, being urged on by their officers, still a couple hundred yards away. He ran to the Minnesotans, saying "We need five minutes! Get me five minutes!" Pointing at the Southern ranks, he ordered "Charge those lines!"

The Minnesotans, 262 men behind the stone wall, adjusted their bayonets, stood up, leaped over the wall and, shouting, ran at the Confederates. No time to reload. It was the most furious hand-to-hand battle in the history of our country. They fought with bayonets, knives, and rifles used as clubs.

The general got his five minutes, the support troops poured onto the ridge, and the South turned back.

There were only 47 Minnesotans still standing where five minutes earlier there had been 262. In five minutes, 215 men

Sergeant Otto Steen, Wisconsin 15th Infantry, Company K

were down, still the record for most men killed and wounded in a single unit in so short a fight.

One of the men wounded was Sergeant Charlie Steen, a musketball through his left thigh. He lost the leg, but he survived, and he came home.

There was a Norwegian among the Confederates who faced Sergeant Steen and the Minnesota First Infantry at Gettysburg. Edward Gunderson from Solor, Norway, had been working on the docks in New Orleans and was drafted. He was wounded in the Gettysburg bayonet attack and he told later how frightening it was to be within yards of Cemetery Ridge and see those 262 gleaming bayonets, a line of bayonets one hundred yards wide, coming at him. After the war, Gunderson became a farmer in Worth County, Iowa.

Three of Charlie Steen's brothers, Theodore, 23, John, 20, and Henry, 18, enlisted together in the Iowa 12th. In the battle at Shiloh, Tennessee, the 12th found itself in the deadliest part of the combat, fighting hand to hand in what came to be known as the Hornet's Nest. While the men of the 12th stubbornly held their ground, regiments on both flanks began falling back, eventually retreating so far that the Iowans were exposed, encircled, and forced to surrender. The Confederates marched their captives, including the three Steen brothers, to Libby Prison in Richmond, Virginia.

Above: Corporal Henry Steen, Iowa 12th Infantry, Company G
Right: Sergeant John Steen, Iowa 12th Infantry, Company G

Another brother, Martin Steen, was 28 when he joined Company E of the 38th Iowa. He took part in the Siege of Vicksburg, the capture of Mobile and many other battles. He was wounded while fighting at Fort Blakely, Alabama.

Otto Steen was the youngest of the six. Just 16, he was said to be the youngest soldier in the all-Norwegian Wisconsin 15th. He was captured in the Battle of New Hope Church, Georgia, and spent nine months in Andersonville prison. When the war ended and prisoners were released, he was little more than a skeleton. He came home to his mother's good cooking, and lived to be 84.

Sergeant Martin Steen, Iowa 38th Infantry, Company E

A Thousand Oles

At least 6,500 Civil War Union soldiers were born in Norway. The exact number may never be known. Vesterheim's database includes men who are listed on military muster rolls, plus dozens more whose descendants have identified the units to which their ancestors belonged. There are another 3,500 names on the Vesterheim list that likely are duplicates of the identified men.

An estimated 300 Norwegians served in Confederate units. There were at least 58 in Texas companies, most being members of town guards that went in as units. None were slave owners.

Wisconsin had the greatest numbers of fighting Norwegians. More than half of all Union soldiers born in Norway enlisted in Wisconsin regiments, 3,609 at last count. The Wisconsin 15th left Madison with 801 men, all Norwegians except for about 30 (three Swedes, three Danes, three Irish, and several officers, surgeons and medical staffers). At least 45 men from Winneshiek County, Iowa, enlisted in Wisconsin's all-Norwegian 15th.

Minnesota had more than 1,200, plus another 200 farmers in and around New Ulm who became citizen soldiers mustered to meet the Sioux.

From Iowa units, 677, of whom 231 were from Winneshiek County.

From Illinois units, 563. There were 56 Norwegians in the Illinois 82nd, an all-immigrant, non-English speaking regiment.

From New York units, 112, most of them from the Bay Ridge section of Brooklyn, serving together in a company in the New York 1st infantry.

The Dakota Territory sent 96 men; 72 were Norwegians.

146 John Johnsons.

46 Hans Hansons.

42 Tom Thompsons.

There were 966 young men named Olson.

199 Ole Olsons.

And a thousand Oles. One of every six Civil War soldiers born in Norway was named Ole.

Brevet Captain Ole K. Hanson,
Wisconsin 15th Infantry, Company A

Peace. Pox. Potatoes.

*So many a fool went over
the sea
Went over to North
America.*

– Henrik Wergeland, in Theodore
C. Blegen, *Norwegian Migration to
America,* vol. 2, Norwegian-
American Historical Association,
1940, p.478.

In old Norway the population was stable. Babies were born, babies died. Adults got sick and died. Food was scarce, poor people generally were hungry and susceptible to diseases. Deaths equaled births. The population was constant. This was true from the time of the Black Death until the nineteenth century.

Then Norway's population exploded.

Why?

Peace. Pox. Potatoes.

Peace. After Napoleon's final defeat, Europe enjoyed relative peace. Fewer young Norwegian men were called south to fight.

Pox. Smallpox every year killed thousands in Norway and throughout Europe, until an English doctor noticed that dairy maids did not get smallpox. They got "cowpox," a mild nonfatal form of smallpox that left them immune to the more dangerous disease. English doctors, and soon doctors everywhere, began vaccinating people, infecting them with cowpox germs.

Potatoes. Potatoes came to Europe from America, from Peru and Brazil actually, and for a time they were largely ignored. No one wanted to eat these lumps from the ground. Until a farmer in France got an idea. He posted a sign in his field threatening court action for anyone who would dig up and

steal his potatoes. Potatoes were 'in.' They would grow anywhere – sandy soil, poor soil, fertile soil, mountain sides with scarce soil. They grew in Ireland. They grew in Norway. And now even poor people could eat their fill.

Norway soon had a rapidly growing population, thanks in great part to its abundant potato crops. Abundant most years, but not all. In 1859 and 1860, there were crop failures over much of the country, and in 1861 a late frost killed that year's harvest. Food again became scarce. Children again began dying, their hunger leaving them too weak to resist pneumonia, tuberculosis, or flu.

Young men and women in Norway's rural areas, children of cotters and itinerant workers, faced bleak futures. A young man might know he could never inherit his father's farm because he was not the eldest. If he were the eldest he would get a farm burdened with mortgages beyond the farm's ability to earn its way out of the debt. Young folks felt honor bound not to stay home eating food their parents could not spare. Older teens had to leave so that younger children would not go hungry.

Where to go?

Letters from America promised rewards for those willing to take risks. Come to America, many of the letters said, land is available, land is cheap, land is fertile.

Thorhaugen, a farm in Gol, Hallingdal

A letter from America arrived in Finmark, Norway, and as was usual, it was passed from home to home. It came from a young man named Bersven Nelson, who had gone to America and had become a soldier in the Wisconsin 15th Infantry. Nelson wrote that he had received one hundred dollars for enlisting, that he was getting clothing and free food, was seeing much of his new country, was being paid $13 a month, and that when his time in the military was up, he would get $50 and 160 acres of land. Pretty enticing to a young man with few opportunities in Norway.[1]

Other letters told of the American enlistment bounty climbing to $300. States added more, as did counties and towns. When President Lincoln called for 300,000 troops, the War Department assigned each state a quota. In one 1862 call, Iowa was told to raise five companies, Winneshiek County to raise two companies. Draft them if you must!

Draft them? Civic pride would not allow that. Newspapers in neighboring towns were trumpeting that their quotas had been filled by volunteers. Would our town do less? Were our boys less patriotic? County officials scrambled to find more bonus money, from taxes, from bonds, from squeezing the merchants along Main Street.

The bounties kept climbing. States added $50 to the $300 federal bonus; counties added $20 to $50, towns tossed in another $5. In some places a volunteer was promised that his wife would get $8 a month while he was gone, and each of his children $4, and that they would be taken care of should he never come back. The enlistee would not receive the bounty money all at once. If a soldier's bounty was $300, he would get $60 at the time of his muster in, another $60 at the end of six months and each six months thereafter. Most young Norwegians chose to have the money held until their discharge. Many took very little – $20 at muster, with the rest held until their discharge.

News of these bounties had many young men in Norway anxious to cross the Atlantic. The American consul in Stockholm, Charles Leas – Sweden and Norway were one country then – told of large numbers of young men crowding into his office seeking to enlist. "They had read of the bounties offered," he said, "and wanted to enlist and use the money to pay for their tickets to America." Leas had to tell them he was not permitted to do that. The U.S. Minister to Sweden-Norway, Jacob Haldeman, wrote that if he had been permitted to pay enlistment bounties he could have in the previous seven months sent three thousand men to the Union Army.

So find the ship fare and let's go. A ticket was cheap – $30 to $60 U.S., about 35 to 70

I bought 80 acres of land... and we cleared 15 acres and seeded 6 acres with winter wheat and built a little house and a cow barn and had 25 acres fenced. I (have) 6 pigs, 9 bushels wheat, 8 chickens and a bit more. I have also bought 2 driving oxen and a four-wheeled vehicle and 2 cows. Furthermore I must tell you how satisfied I am with my emigration. In the beginning, particularly when we were attacked by the illness, all of us, then we were very unhappy in a way words can not describe and many a time we wished we were back in Norway, but now when we are well again, we are very satisfied as the soil is as good as it was described to us.

– Thomas Johnson Lensegrav, Minnesota 3rd Infantry, Company D, from Dunkirk, Dane County, Wisconsin, written April 20, 1846, transcription at Vesterheim from a letter belonging to the family.

Farm in Hallingdal

Norwegian dollars. The price varied depending on the ship. The larger, faster ships charged more – $30 was the best known fare. Children half fare, babies free. Bring your own food and your own blankets.

And there was this new thing Ole was reading about – "homesteading." Any male, 21 or older, could get 160 acres for $13 – $10 of which was for the land and the remaining $3 was for a fee at the land office. He had to live on the land five years, put a hut on it and cultivate a part of it. That was no problem for Ole. He was coming here to stay.

And if there was no other way, Ole could go to the office of the Upper Michigan Mining companies. Agree to work two years and the mining company would buy his ticket for him, give him money for his travel expenses, provide tickets for his wife and children (taking back two-thirds of those expenses out of his future pay). They would pay Ole $260 a year during the time he worked, and provide him a house and food during those two years.

Some historians have written that emigration from Norway fell off drastically during the war years. The United States official immigration records show that in 1861 only 616 Norwegians and Swedes arrived. But the emigration records in Norway show that 8,600 people left for America that year.[2] They came on sailing ships, into St. Lawrence Bay, up river to Quebec, through the Great Lakes to Wisconsin. They never got counted, and a very few who did are shown as entering from Canada.

Ingrid Semmingsen, in her book *Norway to America,* states that nine-tenths of the immigrants coming from Norway during the late 1850s and early 1860s came through Quebec.[3] Norway's emigration records show more people leaving for America in 1860-65 than in 1850-55.

So they came. Vast numbers of young men, willing to take chances that they would survive. Ole Olson, Ole Peterson, Ole Thompson, Ole Johnson, Ole Larson. All those Oles. Following a dream. Seeking a future.

They did survive, often better than non-Norwegian soldiers. Many units in the Union army lost two men to disease for each one killed in action. Among Norwegians that ratio was one to one, actually a bit less. Among men in Andersonville, the infamous prison in Georgia, fewer than one of five captured Union soldiers survived – one of four Norwegians survived. They had been farm boys in Norway. They were farm boys here. They were stronger physically than Yankee lads from America's cities. They were better able to take care of themselves, and more important they had a great will to survive. They had siblings and cousins and sweethearts back in Norway who were counting on them to make it in the new world.

[1] Theodore C. Blegen, *Norwegian Migration to America,* vol. 2, Norwegian-American Historical Association, 1940, p.395.

[2] Ibid., p.386.

[3] Ingrid Semmingsen, *Norway to America: A History of the Migration,* Minneapolis: University of Minnesota Press, 1978, p.57.

And They Were Heroes

When the most celebrated sea battle of the Civil War began on March 9, 1862, in Virginia's Hampton Bay near the mouth of the James River, Norwegian-born Peter Williams didn't know it, but he was about to become a hero.

The South had captured a northern warship called the *Merrimac* and had rebuilt it, covering it with steel plates. Union naval officials had learned of this new warship with its ironclad sides and deck, and they called on John Ericsson, a Swedish inventor, to build an ironclad for the North.

He designed a raft-like vessel that floated low in the water, its deck just over a foot above the waves. Steel plates covered the vessel's sides, from the deck down to three feet below the water line. Amidships, Ericsson put a turret, nine feet high, containing two nine-inch cannons. The turret could be cranked around, allowing the cannons to fire, then cranked around again to protect gunners as they reloaded.

Ericsson's vessel was built in 100 days at a shipyard in Greenpoint, Long Island. They named it the *Monitor*.

On March 6, 1862, a crew of 54 went aboard, and the *Monitor* steamed out of New York to cheers from huge throngs of people gathered on both sides of the East River. Reporters writing about the ship called it a "cheesebox on a raft."

The trip to Hampton Roads, Virginia, took two days. Sounds of battle could be heard as the *Monitor* arrived, the sounds coming from the mouth of the James River, where the *Merrimac*, by then renamed the *Virginia*, was engaging five Northern vessels, including the *Congress* and the *Commodore*. The *Merrimac* sank all five, blasting cannonballs through their wooden sides. The cannonballs fired back at the *Merrimac* bounced harmlessly off the ironclad's sides and deck.

The *Monitor* entered the bay after dark and moved alongside a Union warship, a frigate named *Minnesota*, that was aground on a sandbar.

Early the next morning, a Sunday, the *Merrimac* was seen approaching. The captain of the *Monitor*, John Worden, ordered full steam ahead to put his vessel between the *Merrimac* and the stranded *Minnesota*. Worden and the *Monitor*'s pilot, Quartermaster Peter Williams, were the only members of the vessel's crew able to see out from the ship. They were inside the pilot house, a tiny boxlike structure about a foot high, located forward on the *Monitor*'s flat deck.

The *Merrimac* began firing at the *Minnesota*. The *Monitor* in turn fired at the *Merrimac*. Its first cannonball bounced off the side of the Southern ironclad, but the second went through her superstructure.

A shell from the *Merrimac* slammed into the *Monitor*'s pilot house, wounding Captain Worden. He dropped beside pilot Williams, there to stay throughout the battle because there was not room enough for crew members to reach him.

The *Merrimac* next tried to ram the *Monitor*, but Williams steered his vessel into shallow waters. The *Monitor* could operate in 13 feet of water; the *Merrimac* needed 22. The battle lasted hours, the *Monitor* keeping a position between the *Merrimac* and the *Minnesota*, each of the ironclads shooting at the other. The *Monitor* constantly kept turning, firing, sometimes bumping the larger ship. Neither could do critical damage to the other. The *Merrimac*'s cannonballs bounced off the steel plating. The *Monitor* had better luck; its guns punched two holes in the *Merrimac*'s sides.

After five hours, the tide came in and the *Minnesota* floated free and sailed out of danger. The *Merrimac* gave up the fight and sailed back into the James River under protection of shore batteries.

Williams, who was born in 1831 in Norway, was promoted to master's mate and was awarded the Congressional Medal of Honor for his actions in piloting the *Monitor* in its famous fight.

The *Monitor* went down in a storm off Cape Hatteras on December 31, 1862, and Williams was made an ensign for valorous conduct in his ship's final hours. He was discharged from the Navy in 1867.

Preceding pages: Crewmen on the deck of the *Monitor*. Note the cannonball dents on the turret.
Pilot Peter Williams is seated on the far left, reading a paper.

Seven additional Norwegians were awarded Congressional Medals of Honor during America's Civil War. Six of the eight were sailors; two were soldiers.

Peter Anderson joined the Wisconsin 31st Infantry Regiment at Madison on September 8, 1863. He was awarded his Medal for gallant conduct in saving, entirely unassisted, an artillery piece of the 14th Corps from capture at Bentonville, North Carolina, on March 19, 1865.

John Johnson, who was born in Toten, Norway, enlisted from Janesville into the Wisconsin 2nd Infantry, Company A. He was honored for conspicuous gallantry in the Battle at Antietam. When fellow cannoneers fell during the shelling, he kept on alone, loading, aiming and firing his gun until finally he, too, suffered a severe wound, losing his right arm.

Robert Brown, born in Norway, enlisted from New York in the United States Navy. He was on board the *U.S.S. Richmond* in Mobile Bay on August 5, 1864, serving as a deck officer. According to his citation, he was "cool and courageous at his station throughout the prolonged action. He rendered gallant service as his vessel trained her guns on Fort Morgan and on ships of the Confederacy, despite extremely heavy return fire."

Henry Johnson enlisted in the Navy from New York and served on the *U.S.S. Metacomet*. As a member of the boat's crew, which went to the rescue of the *U.S.S. Tecumseh* when that vessel was struck by a torpedo, he braved intense firing from the enemy forts at Mobile Bay and he aided in rescuing from death ten of the crew of the *Tecumseh*, "eliciting admiration of friend and foe."

Pilot Peter Williams (detail)

William Phinney, another New York sailor born in Norway, won his Medal of Honor in Mobile Bay on August 5, 1864. His vessel, the *U.S.S. Lackawanna,* had been sent out to attack Fort Morgan, Confederate gunboats, and the ram *Tennessee.* Phinney was serving as a gun captain and, according to his citation, showed much presence of mind in managing the gun and in giving much needed encouragement to his crew during the engagement. His actions resulted in the capture of the Confederate ram *Tennessee* and the damaging and destruction of Fort Morgan.

Thomas Robinson, born in Norway, enlisted in the Navy from New York. He was cited for heroic efforts to save from drowning a member of his crew who had fallen overboard.

Augustus Williams, a seaman from Kristiansand, Norway, was aboard the *U.S.S. Santiago de Cuba* during an assault by the Union fleet on Fort Fisher in January, 1865. When the landing party to which he was attached charged the fort with cheers and determination, Williams remained steadfast when, on reaching the foot of the fort, more than two-thirds of the marines and sailors fell back in panic. He took cover when the enemy concentrated its fire on the remainder of his group and, it was said, he alone remained with his executive officer until they could withdraw after dark.

Line engraving of the *Monitor,* 1862

THE ERICSSON STEEL-CLAD BATTERY "MONITOR."

The Mighty 'Little' Wisconsin 15th

Organized at Camp Randall, Madison, Wisconsin's 15th Regiment completed muster into the United States service on February 14, 1862, and left the state for St. Louis, Missouri, on March 2, 1862.

PRESENTED BY THE SOCIETY NORA
of CHICAGO, to the SCANDINAVIEN REGIMENT.
MARCH 1ST, 1862.
"FOR GUD OG VORT LAND!.."

Passing through Chicago, the regiment was presented with a beautiful flag by the Scandinavian "Society Nora." The motto on the flag was, "For God and our country."

On one side was the American colors with gilt stars on a blue field. On the reverse were the American and Norwegian arms, united; the Norwegian arms representing a lion with an axe, on a red field. On the flag was inscribed, "Presented by the Society Nora, of Chicago, to the Scandinavian Regiment, March 1, 1862."

The flag was presented by C. Ditrickson, Esq., accompanied with a speech in the Norwegian language, which was appropriately replied to by Colonel Heg.

— E. B. Quiner, *The Military History of Wisconsin in the War for the Union,* Chicago: Clarke & Co., 1866, p. 614.

Above: The reverse side features 34 stars, the number of states in the Union in 1861.

Opposite: The Nora Society banner, presented to the Wisconsin 15th as it marched through Chicago on March 1, 1862.

Colonel Hans Christian Heg

No Union soldier born in Norway is more famous than Colonel Hans Heg. He commanded the all-Norwegian Wisconsin 15th Regiment. He was respected by his men for his fairness. They admired his courage, confident that in the most dangerous battles he would be as far forward as they, as defiant of Confederate bullets as he expected them to be.

Had he lived a few days longer than he did, he would have become a brigadier general, for he was commanding a brigade when he died.

Hans Heg was born at Lier, near Drammen, Norway, on December 21, 1829. He came to America at age 11. His father, Even Heg, settled his family in Norway Township, Racine County, Wisconsin. Even Heg, with two others, published *Nordlyset* (Northern Light), the first Norwegian language newspaper in America.

Young Hans grew up around the politicians who came to the newspaper office in Muskego, and long before he was old enough to vote, he had developed an interest in the politics of his day. He became an antislavery Democrat while still in his teens.

In 1849, he went off to California to look for gold, found no more than a thousand dollars over his expenses the first year, and a bit more the second year. Then came news that his father had died. His mother had died a few years earlier. Hans returned to Wisconsin to manage the family farm and care for his siblings.

He married a neighbor girl, Gunhild Einung, and determined to spend the rest of his life as a farmer. But he could not stay out of politics. He was soon holding one office after another: county supervisor, justice of the peace, assessor, county director of the poor. These activities left little time for farming and, in 1859, he gave it up and moved to Waterford to run a store.

He had not given up politics, and he was soon nominated for the post of state prison commissioner. He campaigned enthusiastically and was elected.

He instituted many prison reforms, including having his prisoners make furniture for all of the state's charitable institutions. His name soon became known throughout Wisconsin, and in 1861 he was again nominated.

He began to remind friends of his antislavery sentiments and that he wanted to be in the war. He went to the governor and got permission to raise a regiment of Norwegian immigrants to fight as infantry. He received his commission on December 21, 1861, effective from September 30 of that year.

Heg threw himself into recruiting, traveling throughout Wisconsin and into adjoining counties in Illinois, Iowa, and Minnesota. "To arms for the defense of our Union," he proclaimed. "The government of our adopted country is in danger."[1] He was successful. Young men were eager to join a unit where all others would be like them, Norwegians.

Colonel Hans Heg, commander of the Wisconsin 15th

By February 14, 1862, he was in Madison, organizing the all-Norwegian 15th Infantry Volunteers. His men got their uniforms and muskets, a few days of training, and on March 1, 1862, they headed south.

On September 26, 1862, Colonel Heg wrote his wife, telling of marching through Louisville, Kentucky. He said, "My regiment went through singing Norwegian songs and attracted more attention that any other regiment that passed."[2]

Heg led his men through several battles with few losses. After the battle of Knob Gap he wrote, "I charged with my regiment up to a battery and captured one brass cannon, seven horses, three prisoners and one caisson; – and what is best of all – not one man was wounded."[3]

Heg's military history puts him as commander of a fort at Bird's Point, for two months commander of Mississippi River Island No. 10, and leading his regiment on its march to Corinth, Mississippi, and through Florence and Murfreesboro, Tennessee, to Nashville. The regiment lost heavily at Fort Donelson and at Shiloh.

In the Buell Campaign and in the Battle of Stones River, Heg's bravery under fire attracted the attention of his superiors.

General Rosecrans transferred Heg and his 15th to the Third Brigade and made Heg the brigade commander. In the Battle at Chickamauga, he was assigned to put a bridge over the Tennessee River and to lead his men across.

O. A. Buslett, in his book *Det Femtende Wisconsin* (The Fifteenth Wisconsin) tells what happened:

> The colonel was under heavy fire the whole time, and when the troops were forced to fall back, he waved his hat and shouted that they should follow him, and it had an electric effect; they stormed the enemy and drove him back six hundred feet, before the superiority of the enemy's force became too great.[4]

A reporter writing in a Cincinnati newspaper told of watching the Norwegian 15th at Chickamauga. "Bullets tore through the ranks; grape and cannister flew whistling among the brave men, but they stood their ground, not yielding an inch."[5]

Half the regiment, 302 men, were killed, died of wounds, or were taken prisoner. One was Colonel Heg himself, shot from his horse late on the first day of the battle.

Buslett describes Heg's fall:

> He came unscathed out of the fire; it was a stray graze that felled him. He had just spurred his horse to ride to another part of the line when he fell off; he climbed back up again, but when he had gotten into the saddle he fell forward over his horse's neck. He could not hold himself upright any longer.[6]

Heg slid from his saddle and a sergeant, Lars Larson of Company K, ran to him, ignoring the bullets and musketballs that buzzed past. Larson caught the colonel, half-carried him from the battlefield, and got him to a sheltered area among nearby trees, where others could help. Sergeant Larson then raced back into the thick of the fighting and was himself wounded and taken prisoner by the Confederates. After the war Larson received an honorary commission for his bravery.

In the town of Norway in Racine County, Wisconsin, a well-to-do farmer named Even Heg built a huge barn which he offered for church services and community events. He also used it as sleeping quarters for newcomers arriving from Norway.

Many young men enlisting in the Union Army gave Norway, Wisconsin, as their American place of residence.

There is a cannonball monument to Heg in Georgia where he died. There is a statue of him before the state capitol in Madison; one in Muskego, Wisconsin, where he lived; and one in Norway at Lier near Drammen, where he was born.

Some Came from Illinois

Eighty-nine young men born in Norway and living in Illinois went up to Madison, Wisconsin, to become soldiers in the all-Norwegian 15th Regiment led by Colonel Hans Heg. Seventy-two of them were from the city of Chicago, 14 were from around Rockford.

Besides the 89 young Norwegian men, there were 563 others who enlisted in Illinois regiments. Fifty-six of those joined the Illinois 82nd, an all-immigrant, non-English speaking regiment.

Kiler Jones of Quincy, Illinois, was not Norwegian, but his wife was. Jones was commissioned a lieutenant colonel on December 21, 1861, and was authorized by the governor of Wisconsin to help raise a regiment of Norwegians and Swedes. He supervised the organization of the several companies. It had been understood that the 15th Regiment would be commanded by Hans Heg, who was still serving as Wisconsin's state prison commissioner. Jones was to be the regiment's lieutenant commander. It never happened. On March 1, his commission was revoked, due – according to historian E. B. Quiner – to "some unfortunate misunderstanding."[7] The regiment left Wisconsin without a lieutenant colonel. Jones eventually moved up to Manitowoc, Wisconsin.

A Chicago police officer named Andrew Torkildsen opened a recruiting office on North Wells Street and enlisted Norwegians in the Wisconsin 15th. They became Company A, with Torkildsen the company captain. His company became known as the St. Olaf Rifles.

Fredrik Fleischer was one of the Company A Chicagoans. He was born at Gudvangen, in Voss, Norway, and was one of the first men signed up by Kiler Jones. He became a corporal. In August 1863, he was given a discharge so he could go back to Norway and claim an inheritance, his family's hotel. He had to hire a substitute to take his place and found a man named Hubbard Hammock, who was willing to do that. Hammock served the remainder of Fleischer's enlistment. He was severely wounded at Chickamauga, but survived.

Edward Holberg, Niels Knudsen, and Olaf Olson, three Chicago boys, were among several soldiers who wound up under arrest following a *Syttende Mai* celebration held in 1862 on Mississippi River Island No. 10. Most of the celebrants were released the next morning. These three faced more serious charges and one, Niels Knudsen, managed to escape in July and was never caught. It is said that he went to Texas.

Anthony Oyen, a pharmacist from Bodø, Norway, was one of the first Chicagoans to enlist. He served as a hospital pharmacist, was captured at Chickamauga, and served 18 months in Confederate prisons, including Andersonville. He survived, came home, and served 20 years as a Chicago policeman.

Come, then, young Norsemen, and take part in defending our country's cause, and thus fulfill a pressing duty which everyone who is able to do so owes to the land in which he lives. Let us band together and deliver untarnished to posterity the old honorable name of Norsemen.

– Col. Hans Heg, recruiting young men to serve in his all-Norwegian regiment, in *Emigraten*, November 18, 1861, quoted in Theodore C. Blegen, *The Civil War Letters of Hans Christian Heg,* Northfield: Norwegian-American Historical Association, 1936, p.23.

Two men, both named Gabriel Somme, both from Chicago, were likely father and son, since one was 43, the other 22. The older Somme was in a Confederate prison, but survived the war; the younger died of disease on Island No. 10.

Samuel and Thomas Sampson, young brothers from Boone County, Illinois, enlisted together, mustered at Madison together, and died within a week of each other, of disease, at Island No. 10. They are buried in the National Cemetery at Memphis.

Ole Knudsen Hanson from Seljord, Telemark, came to America at age five. He lived in Boone County, Illinois, but came down to Chicago and enlisted in the Wisconsin 15th. He was wounded in the battle of New Hope Church and left on the battlefield, where Confederate troops picked him up and held him until the end of the war. He was crippled the rest of his life. A citation given him said that "although wounded five times, Ole Knudsen Hanson refused to leave the field and finally fell into the hands of the enemy, he having advanced so far forward it was impossible for his Regiment to reach and save him."

Camp Randall, in Madison, Wisconsin, served as the training ground for many Wisconsin regiments, including the 15th.

CAMP RANDALL, (MADISON. WIS.,) AS IT APPEARED IN 1862.

15t WIS. REG. CAMP ON ISLAND NUMBER 10 TENN

The camp on Island No. 10, drawn by Private Ole R. Dahl of Company H

Island No. 10

The first major military action for the all-Norwegian Wisconsin 15th was the siege of Island No. 10, so named because it was the tenth Mississippi River island south of the Ohio River.

It was a small island, about 200 acres, located 50 miles downstream from Cairo, Illinois. Confederate batteries had a clear view upstream, and could easily keep vessels from sailing past. (The island no longer exists; spring floods have washed it away.)

Colonel Heg's regiment, along with the 27th Illinois, laid siege to the island on March 15, 1862. On April 7, Confederate forces evacuated, leaving behind large stores of ammunition and about a hundred horses and mules. Troops who came onto the island found conditions unhealthy and soon moved to higher ground on the Kentucky shore. All the men, both the healthy and the sick, lived in tents.

On Island No. 10, the Wisconsin 15th only lost one man who died of wounds (Johan Black), and only one more who died in an accident (Aaron Merchant of G Company), but 162 men fell sick and were unable to fight.

Of those 162, 42 died on the island; 46 became disabled and were given discharges and sent home; and 74, who were in hospitals, had to be left behind when the regiment moved on. Some of those discharged died soon after. Of the 74 left on the island, about half recovered and rejoined their regiment.

There were 801 men in the 15th when the regiment left Madison on March 2. Eight of the regiment's ten companies left Island No. 10 on June 12; two companies, G and I, stayed until October to garrison the island.

The ailment most common on Island No. 10 was diarrhea. O. A. Buslett, writing in *Det Femtende Regiment*, blames the Mississippi River water. He said the water was especially dangerous when stirred up and, even settled, it still was full of foreign matter. Diarrhea became chronic and doctors were at a loss to treat it. Victims strong enough to travel were given discharges and sent home, most of them to die later.[8]

There were other diseases affecting men of the 15th. "Nerve fever" was one, a term referring to both typhus and typhoid fevers. Erysipelas was a sometimes fatal skin infection caused by streptococcus bacteria. Tuberculosis and measles were widespread, especially during winter. Typhoid and measles were especially to be dreaded, for most of those victims died.

After the battle of Corinth, the post at Mississippi River Island No. 10 lost its importance. Eight companies of the Wisconsin 15th were ordered to join the main army. Left behind were about 150 men, including companies G and I of the 15th and L of the Second Illinois Cavalry. This garrison was moved from the island to the river bank, where sentries could watch over the river and flooded marshy areas.

When the island had been captured, several hundred prisoners had been gathered in, but many Southern soldiers had hidden in small

Lieutenant Nils J. Gilbert, Wisconsin 15th Infantry, Company A

Nils J. Gilbert, in a letter home from Mississippi River Island No. 10, told of celebrating Norway's 17th of May holiday. The men had ordered kegs of beer from a supplier in Cairo, Illinois. "Our company," he said, "got a barrel and a half."

He said the men discharged thirteen cannon shots, marched in a parade, and then drank the beer "freely and happily."

– Letter dated May 20, 1862, quoted in O.A. Buslett, *The Fifteenth Wisconsin by O.A. Buslett,* trans., Barbara C. Scott, 1999, p.395, available from the State Historical Society of Wisconsin. Originally published as O.A. Buslett, *Det Femtende Regiment,* Decorah: B. Anundsen, 1894.

timber hideouts and among the local inhabitants. Because of the sentries, they could not get to the mainland without being seen and captured.

Soon came reports from abandoned slaves in the area that many of the Confederates hidden on the island were escaping and that there was a secret passageway they were using.

First Sergeant Charles Nelson of Company G decided he would find out how the men were getting away. With his commander's permission, he dressed himself in captured Confederate clothing, so as to pass himself off as a member of the Memphis Light Artillery. Then he went to the island and became a Confederate anxious to get out of range of the Yanks.

Nelson soon found a ferryman named "Little Bob" Thompson, who along with his father, "Big Bob," had been rowing Southern soldiers across at night. Nelson took advantage of Little Bob's generosity, made his way back to his company and the next day showed up again, this time in his Union uniform and leading a squad of Company G troops.

Little Bob went to prison. Sergeant Nelson was promoted to lieutenant.

The Battle at Rocky Face Ridge

The mountain blocking the Union advance on Atlanta was called Birds' Roost. It is high and its slopes are steep. Confederate troops were on top, determined to keep the Northerners from reaching the town of Dalton and the city of Atlanta. On May 7, 1864, General William Sherman's army was drawn up in front of the mountain, its vanguard against the foot of the mountain, so close that the Confederate troops on top amused themselves by rolling stones down on the men below.

The Wisconsin 15th was in the middle at the base of the mountainside called Rocky Face Ridge. Sherman ordered an attack.

Sergeant John Wrolstad of Company I was chosen to lead. Very early the next morning, Wrolstad and his squad stripped off their haversacks, caps, and canteens, taking only rifles, knives and a few rounds of ammunition.

Silently they began to climb, slipping hands and feet into crevices and clefts, clutching at brush and bushes that grew on the mountain face. As each man moved up a little, he would lean over, reach back down and pull up the man below him – all in silence.

Finally they gained the top. Sergeant Wrolstad was the first man up. He gathered his squad around him and they fell upon the sleeping Southern soldiers.

The fighting was severe and short. Wrolstad's men soon controlled the mountaintop and Sherman's army marched past.

Sergeant John Olson Wrolstad,
Wisconsin 15th Infantry, Company I

With the taking of Atlanta the most important part of the 15th's history is over... For more than two years it had shared the troubles and triumphs of the Cumberland Army, its defeats and its victories. It had, before this army got its name, marched with it through Tennessee and Kentucky during the difficult campaign of 1862; it had fought together with it at Perryville, Knob Gap, Stones River, Chickamauga, and Missionary Ridge; it had taken part in the winter campaign in the mountains of East Tennessee and now in the last major campaign had distinguished itself at Rocky Face Ridge, New Hope Church, and innumerable skirmishes. If ever any living soul were to come home from "the little 15th," it was about time that they left.

- O.A. Buslett, *The Fifteenth Wisconsin by O.A. Buslett,* trans., Barbara C. Scott, 1999, p.202, available from State Historical Society of Wisconsin. Originally published as O.A. Buslett, *Det Femtende Regiment,* Decorah: B. Anundsen, 1894.

[1] *Emigraten*, October 7, 1861, quoted in Theodore C. Blegen, *The Civil War Letters of Hans Christian Heg,* Northfield: Norwegian-American Historical Society, 1936, p.23.

[2] Theodore C. Blegen, *The Civil War Letters of Hans Christian Heg,* Northfield: Norwegian-American Historical Society, 1936, p.140.

[3] Ibid., p.35.

[4] O.A. Buslett, *The Fifteenth Wisconsin by O.A. Buslett,* trans., Barbara C. Scott, 1999, p.202, available from State Historical Society of Wisconsin. Originally published as O.A. Buslett, *Det Femtende Regiment,* Decorah: B. Anundsen, 1894.

[5] Blegen, op. cit., p.39.

[6] Buslett, op. cit., p.202.

[7] E. B. Quiner, *The Military History of Wisconsin in the War for the Union,* Chicago: Clarke & Co., 1866. p. 614.

[8] Buslett, op. cit., pp. 123-4.

Song sheet from a regimental song –
Note that the melody is a Norwegian tune.

The Volunteer Soldier of the 15th Wisconsin.

MEL: DEN GANG JEG DROG AFSTED.

I shan't forget that day
When first I went away—
Me lassie, dear, she would not stay!
Of course she would not stay!
    You cannot go along,
    Through warfare, strife and throng,
But if they don't kill me, dear, I shall return with song;
  I would, was there no danger, Sis, as lief remain with thee,
But all the girls of North, you see, rely just now on me,
        And therefore I will fight
        The rebels left and right.
            Hurrah! hurrah! hurrah!

Our folks at home, they thought—
The dear old folks at home—
That all their chaps, not ought to leave,
For fear they might be caught:
    If all our hands go 'way,
    The enemy to slay,   [the hay?
Why, who shall plow the corn fields, then, and who shall move
  Well, there is just the reason, Sis, why we must all go in,
For else the rebels certainly would come and do the thing.
        And therefore we will fight
        These rebels left and right.
            Hurrah! hurrah! hurrah!

We're bound for sunny South—
Ho hah! for sunny South—
To tell them what's the truth, and shout
It at the muskets mouth.
    And if they won't believe
    Plain truth, they shall receive
A dose of pills and powder, which, I think, will them relieve.
  A lesson we will teach them, in cities large and small,
Till our beloved stars and stripes are floating over all.
        Yes, therefore will we fight
        The rebels left and right.
            Hurrah! hurrah! hurrah!

Claus L. Clausen, a prominent immigrant pastor who organized the first Norwegian Lutheran congregation in the United States in Muskego, Wisconsin. He served as chaplain for the Wisconsin 15th. Company K is named for him.

The Men of the Wisconsin 15th

The Companies of the Wisconsin 15th Regiment

A St. Olaf's Rifles
(The Chicago Company)

B The Wergeland Guards
(Named for Norwegian poet, songwriter, and playwright)

C Norway Bear Hunters

D Norway Wolf Hunters
(The Waupun Company)

E Odin's Rifles

F K.K.'s Protectors
(The Valdres Company, named after Col. Kiler K. Jones)

G Rock River Rangers

H Heg's Rifles
(The Voss Company)

I The Scandinavian Mountaineers
(The Waupaca Company)

K Clausen's Guards
(Named for the first chaplain of the 15th)

The 42 Men Who Died of Disease on Island No. 10

Name	Company
AMUNDSON, Engebret	K
ANDERSON, Anton	G
ANDERSON, Christopher	G
ANDERSON, Halvor	B
ANDERSON, Hans	G
ASLAKSON, Torger	K
BENJAMIN, Ambrose	G
BERG, Lars	H
BERGSLI, Lars	?
CHRISTIANSEN, Mathias	G
CHRISTIANSON, Ole	F
CHRISTOPHERSON, Frank	H
CHRISTOPHERSON, Ole	E
DAHL, Ole	E
DOKKEN, Knud	H
FRANSEN, Hans	?
GRELL, John	F
HALVORSON, Lars	B
HELGESON, Gulbrand	K
JOHNSON, John H.	B
JORGANSON, Gunder	F
KNUDSON, Erick	H
LANFELL, Hans	G
LARSON, Gunder	K
MOE, Jens	B
MOE, Ole	?
NIELSON, Haakon	G
NIELSON, Jacob	C
NIELSON, Lars	?
OLSON, Albert	I
OSGOOD, James	G
RUSTE, Christian	E
SAMPSON, Samuel	A
SAMPSON, Thomas	A
SETTER, John	G
SKJELDE, Ole	B
SYVERSON, Knud	F
THOMPSON, Andrew	H
THOMPSON, Lewis	A
THORSTEN, Gilbert	G
TORGERSON, Anders	G
VIKINGSON, Knut	?

The 46 Men Who Fell Sick on Island No. 10 and Were Discharged

Name	Company	Name	Company
ANDERSON, Ole	G	LARSON, Lars	G
ANDREASON, Oluf	I	LOVE, Jeremiah	G
BENTLY, William	G	NELSON, Edgar	G
BERG, Anders	F	NELSON, John	K
BOASON, Anton	I	NIELSON, Niels	C
BORCHSENIUS, Hans	B	OGLESON, Lewis	G
BROWN, Fredrick	A	OLSON, Hans	I
BURK, Edward	C	OLSON, Jacob	K
ELLINGBOE, Helge	F	OLSON, Knud	G
ERIKSON, Lewis	E	OLSON, Lars	K
HALLING, Lars	E	OLSON, Nels	D
HALVORSON, Guttorm	D	OLSON, Tolloff	I
HALVORSON, Helge	I	PAGE, George	C
HALVORSON, Lars	I	PETERSON, Christian	C
HANSON, Andrew	I	PETERSON, John	I
HILL, Edward	G	RAMBECK, John	I
HILL, Horace	G	REEVES, William	C
INGEBRETSON, Julius	I	SANDSMARK, Aadne	E
JACKSON, Jacob	I	SIMENSEN, Johannes	G
JOHNSON, Carl	C	SUNBY, Christopher	H
JOHNSON, Svend	D	TORGERSON, Steven	H
JORGENSON, Lars	I	ULEN, Ole	K
KITTELSON, Paul	I	WHITCOMB, Henry	C

The 20 Men Who Were Sick While on Island No. 10, But Were Able to Return to Duty and Move Out with the Regiment

Name	Company	Name	Company
AMUNDSON, Arne	G	LARKEE, John	B
ELLEFSON, Anders	B	LERUM, Hans	H
ERICKSON, Ellend	K	MJELDE, Knud	B
GROSHONG, William	C	MONSEN, Anton	A
HANSEN, Christen	B	NELSON, Lars	C
HANSON, Hans	G	OLSON, Halvor	D
JOHNSON, John	B	OLSON, Nils	D
JOHNSON, Ole	G	OLSON, Sven	H
JOHNSON, Soren	I	SORENSON, Hans	C
KITTLESON, Knud	D	SWENSON, Bernt	G

The 74 Men Sick in Camp Hospitals Who Were Left Behind on Island No. 10 When the Regiment Moved On

Name	Company		Name	Company	
AGAR, Gabriel	H	Died	KAMMEN, Fredrick	D	
ANDERSON, Martin	D		KNUDSON, Christian	H	
ANDERSON, Torvald	H		LAGESON, Hans	B	
ANONSON, Kittel	B		LARSON, Halvor	H	
ARNESON, Lawrence	E		LARSON, Stark	B	
CHRISTENSON, Hans	F		LOGEN, Tobias	E	
CHRISTOPHERSON, Fingal	K		LOKKEN, Ole	H	
CHRISTOPHERSON, Ole	E	Died	MATHIASON, Mathias	C	
DAHL, Ivar	K		MIKKELSON, Ole	K	
ERIKSON, Helge	K	Died	MORK, Ole	K	
ESPELIE, Helge	E		NILSON, Iver	K	
EVENSON, Erick	H		NILSON, Lauris	K	
FOSS, Syver	E		OLSON, Gudmon	F	
GILBERT, Gulbrand	F		OLSON, Gustav	F	
GULBRANDSON, Christopher	K		OLSON, Helge	K	
GUNDHUS, Christian	E	Died	OLSON, Ingebrigt	H	Died
HALVORSON, Even	H		OLSON, Kittel	K	
HALVORSON, Halvor	B	Died	OLSON, Knud	K	
HALVORSON, Nels	H		OLSON, Lars	E	
HANSON, Andrew	I		OLSON, Mical	A	Died
HANSON, Jens	E		OPPEN, Tosten	F	Died
HANSON, Mathias	K		PEDERSON, Hans	D	Died
HANSON, Niri	E		PEDERSON, Narve	K	Died
HELGESON, Arne	K		PETERS, John	E	
HELGESON, Ole	H		RASMUSSON, Aslak	K	Died
HELGESON, Peder	K		RULLAND, Osten	E	
HOLAND, Thomas	D	Died	SACHARIASON, Asbjorn	E	
HOVERUD, Ole	E		SANDER, Bernt	K	Died
INGEBRETSON, Tobias	A		SANVIG, Thomas	H	
IVERSON, Ole	H		SEBJORNSON, Lars	K	
JACOBSON, Jacob	D		SEVERSON, Johannes	K	
JOHNSON, Andrew	H		SIME, Edlen	H	
JOHNSON, Gulbrand	E	Died	SYVERSON, Bryngel	E	
JOHNSON, John	A		THOMPSON, Lars	H	
JOHNSON, Osmund	H		THOMPSON, Thomas	F	
JORGENSON, Lars	K		TRAAEN, Herbrand	H	Died
JORGENSON, Martin	A		TRONDSON, Gilbert	F	Died

Ole Olson

There were fifteen men named "Ole Olson" in the Wisconsin 15th Regiment, five of them in Company F.

Andersonville

One hundred eleven men born in Norway became prisoners of war in Andersonville, the infamous prison in Georgia in which all prisoners starved and few survived. Most had been captured at Chickamauga.

Of the 111, 76 died there. Forty-nine of the 76 who died were from the Wisconsin 15th Infantry Regiment. There were 63 men from the 15th Wisconsin in the prison; 14 of those survived.

The number of deaths as reported inside the prison was about 100 per day for the month of August. Dysentery and scurvy were the principal ailments. We were not allowed wood enough to cook what little they gave us, although there was plenty of timber in sight. Our men would fight among themselves for a chance to carry out our dead so as to pick a few sticks of wood up and bring back with them. I helped carry out one man – forgot his name. Pat Sadge helped carry him out to the Dead House, which was a large tent. But who could describe the sight which met our eyes? There were 40 or 50 dead men lying there side by side, many with their eyes partly open, their hands crossed and tied, their toes tied together, a slip of paper pinned to their breast with name, company and regiment written on. From here the rebels hauled them by wagon load and buried them in trenches.

– John Stortz, Co. A, 2nd Batt., 16th U.S.Infantry, Decorah Ia., "Experiences of a Prisoner During the Civil War In and Out of the Hands of the Rebels," *Annals of Iowa*, vol. 37, no. 3, 1964, p.169

Norwegian Soldiers Who Died in Andersonville Prison

Wisconsin 15th Infantry

Name	Company	Enlistment Address
BJORNSON, Nils	I	Spring Prairie, Wis.
BRANDSTAD, George	A	Chicago, Ill.
BRITTON, Harvey	B	Racine County, Wis.
BRUNES, Olaus	G	Belleville, Wis.
BURKE, Ole	B	La Crosse, Wis.
CHRISTENSON, Tobias	A	La Crosse, Wis.
ENGER, Jens	K	Fillmore County, Minn.
ERICKSON, Christian	?	Wis.
ERICKSON, Christopher	B	Black Earth, Wis.
ERICKSON, S.	D	?
FEGAN, Michael	I	Cairo, Ill.
FERGUSON, F.	G	?
GJERDE, Andrew	H	Deerfield, Wis
*GRUND, Louis	I	Stockholm, Wis.
GUNDERSON, Hans	I	Scandinavia, Wis.
HALDORSON, Ole	F	Gjerpen, Wis.
HANSON, Jens	K	Calumet County, Wis.
HANSON, Lars	B	Stoughton, Wis.
HAUNES, Ole	H	Clermont, Iowa
HENDERSON, P.	F	?
HOFLAND, Halvor	K	Winnneshiek County, Iowa
JACOBSON, Ole	D	New Lisbon, Wis.
JOHNSON, John	C	Racine County, Wis.
JOHNSON, Ole	F	Manitowoc, Wis.
KNUDSON, Christian	K	Fillmore County, Minn.

* Born in Sweden.

Wisconsin 15th Infantry, continued

Name	Company	Enlistment Address
KNUDSON, J.	E	?
LARSON, Mads	B	Stoughton, Wis.
LODGAARD, Elias	A	Chicago, Ill.
MYHRE, Simon	I	Waupaca County, Wis.
NELSON, Knud	H	Leeds Centre, Wis.
OLESON, Oliver	B	?
OLSEN, Ole M.	B	Black Earth, Wis.
OLSON, Michael	B	Stoughton, Wis.
OPDAHL, John	B	Leeds, Wis.
PEDERSON, Arel	K	Worth County, Iowa
PEDERSON, Sever	K	Winneshiek County, Iowa
PEDERSON, Soren	K	Walworth County, Wis.
PETERSON, A.	K	?
PETERSON, C.	I	?
PETERSON, Ole	I	Waupaca County, Wis.
PETERSON, Simon	I	Scandinavia, Wis.
RAMBECK, John	I	New Hope, Wis.
STEFFES, Reinart	F	Manitowoc County, Wis.
THOMPSON, C.	K	?
THOMPSON, Christian	E	Spring Grove, Minn.
THORESON, Fingar	G	Rock County, Wis.
TORGERSON, Torger	G	Beloit, Wis.
WESTBY, O. P.	I	?
WISTE, Ole	?	?

49 total

Other Units

Name	Company	Enlistment Address
AAS, Paul	Ill. 89th Inf. Co. D	Chicago, Ill.
ANDERSON, Andrew	N.Y. 100th Inf.	Door County, Wis.
EMMONSON, John	Ill. 16th Inf. Co. L	Galesburg, Ill.
ERICKSEN, C.	Ill. 16th Cav. Co. M	?
FERGUSON, W.	Wis. 24th Inf. Co. D	?
GILBERT, Ole	Wis. 10th Inf. Co. K	Waupun, Wis.
HALVORSEN, Peter	Minn. 9th Inf. Co. D	Oshawa, Minn.
HANSON, Jens	Iowa 12th Inf. Co. B	Winneshiek County, Iowa
HANSON, Knud	Wis. 1st Cav. Co. F	Winchester, Wis.
HANSON, Matthew	Wis. 1st Inf. Co. B	Manitowoc, Wis.
HAUFF, Matthew	Wis. 10th Inf. Co. K	Hortonville, Wis.
JACKSON, I.	Wis. 14th Inf. Co. B	?
JOHNSON, Nils	Minn. 9th Inf. Co. H	Carver, Minn.
JOHNSON, W.	Wis. 6th Inf. Co. H	?
MATHISON, E.H.	Wis. 2nd Cav. Co. C	?
MOEN, O.M.	?	?
MUGEDALEN, Ole	?	?
OLSON, John	Ill. 89th Inf. Co. D	Chicago, Ill.
PATTERSON, J.	Wis. 21st Inf. Co. A	?
STARR, Charles	Iowa 30th Inf. Co. H	Glendale, Iowa
STOREN, Alexander	Ill. 89th Inf. Co. D	Chicago, Ill.
THOMPSON, D.D.	Wis. 36th Inf. Co. B	?
THORSON, Peter	Wis. 24th Inf. Co. G	Milwaukee, Wis.
TORKELSEN, Neil	Iowa 16th Inf. Co. H	Decorah, Iowa
WANG, Andreas	?	?
WESLEY, Ole	?	?
YESSON, Alexander	Wis. 24th Inf. Co. A	Milwaukee, Wis.

27 total

Norwegian Soldiers Who Survived Their Time in Andersonville Prison

Wisconsin 15th Infantry

Name	Company	Enlistment Address
AMONDSON, Arne	G	Clinton, Wis.
BRANSTAD, Ole	A	Milwaukee, Wis.
ERICKSON, G.	?	Wis.
GILBERT, E.H.	E	?
GLEASON, J.	C	?
HALVORSON, Hans	D	Neenah, Wis.
HANSON, Ole K.	A	Boone County, Ill.
HANSON, Ole	K	Walworth County, Wis.
JOHNSON, Osmund	K	Fillmore County, Minn.
JOHNSON, Peter	C	?
MADSON, Bernt	B	Cambridge, Wis.
OYEN, Anthony	?	Chicago, Ill.
STEEN, Otto	K	Decorah, Iowa
STEENSLAND, Ole	E	Iowa County, Wis.

14 total

Other Units

Name	Company	Enlistment Address
ANDERSON, Magnus	Iowa 27th Inf. Co. B	Lansing, Iowa
ARNEGAARD, Ole	?	?
ASLAKSON, Burn	Minn. 9th Inf. Co. H	Carver County, Minn.
BERGH, Peter	Minn. 1st Inf.	?
HAARVEI, Knud	?	?
HALVORSON, Torbjorn	Wis. 12th Inf. Co. A	Martell, Wis.
HOFF, John	?	Minn.
JOHNSON, Andrew	?	?
LERUM, John	?	Minn.
LUNDBERG, Peter	Minn. 3rd Inf. Co. D	?
MADISON, Knut	?	?
MARINDAHL, Peter	?	?
MYRAH, Hans	Minn.	Spring Grove, Minn.
OLSEN, Anton	?	?
ORSLAND, Herbrand	N.Y. 151st Inf.	Kendall, N.Y.
PAULSEN, Gilbert	?	?
SPORKLAND, Edward	?	Wis.
SWANSON, Christopher	Minn. 9th Inf. Co. C	Mower County, Minn.
TOLLEFSON, Andreas	?	Fillmore County, Minn.
TVINGLE, Chris	?	?
WILSON, Ole	?	?

21 total

To Each One His Story

Perhaps more telling than vivid descriptions of battles, or long lists of those who fought and died, are the personal stories of the men and women who immigrated to a New World only to be caught up in a civil war unparalleled in history. Here are just a few of those stories.

Lars Knudsen Aaker

Lars Knudsen Aaker of Red Wing came from Lærdal in Telemark. He was in the Minnesota legislature when the war began. He resigned his seat and went into the state's 3rd Infantry as a second lieutenant. He moved up to Alexandria after the war.

Ole Anderson and Mary Katterud, a Love Story

A great love story of the American Civil War is that of Ole Anderson and Mary Katterud, each born in Norway, each growing up on the American frontier.

Ole, a nephew of a pioneer pastor named Nils Brandt, was said to be the most popular young man in Decorah, Iowa. He was tall, handsome, blond, well mannered, well liked by other teens and by adults of the town. It was said that the mother of every teenage girl in Decorah had her cap set on winning Ole for her daughter.

Mary, daughter of Nils Hanson Katterud, lived on a farm near Decorah. Elisabeth Koren, wife of another pioneer pastor, kept a diary and in it often wrote of Mary, that she was bright and pretty and most willing to help others. Mary came frequently to the Koren home to do housework, pull garden weeds, and play with the Koren baby.

At 15, Mary won a Jenny Lind scholarship. The famous 'Swedish Nightingale,' in agreeing to an American concert tour, had insisted that showman P. T. Barnum fund scholarships for Scandinavian girls. Mary used her scholarship at Platteville Academy, a teachers' school in Wisconsin. She came home a year later and became Winneshiek County's first public school teacher.

Ole and Mary met, fell in love and agreed to marry. Their betrothal, as was the custom in the mid 1800s, was announced in their church. Mary began planning their wedding.

Then came the war and President Lincoln's call for troops. The Decorah Guards immediately volunteered. They elected officers and chose Ole Anderson to be their lieutenant. They marched away to become Company D in the Iowa 3rd Infantry.

The 3rd soon found itself south of Liberty, Missouri, at a place called Blue Mills, 600 men in all, facing a Confederate force of 4,000. Letters sent home by men who were in that battle tell of the fighting, of the order to charge, of the men running forward, Lieutenant Anderson out in front, turning to urge his men on. He took a musketball in the side of his head and fell as his men swept over him.

The battle raged through the day and the Confederates gradually pushed the Union troops back to where they had been before the fighting began.

At dawn the Southerners began gathering the dead and wounded. A burial cart rattled across from the Confederate lines. Its driver said, "There seems to be some life in this one."

It was the lieutenant, Ole Anderson. The Southerners returned him to the Northern troops, and Northern hands lifted him to an ambulance wagon. He was taken to a Union hospital where he lay unconscious, day after day. After three weeks, he opened his eyes.

Eleven months later, they led Ole from the hospital, the Confederate musketball still in his temple. They put a discharge paper in his hands and sent him home, a broken man, mentally shaken, never to recover. They sent him home to Iowa, home to Mary.

Lieutenant Ole A. Anderson, Iowa 3rd Infantry, Company D

The State of Iowa.

To all to Whom These Presents shall Come–Greeting:

KNOW YE, *That having* *Ole A. Anderson having* *been duly* *Elected* *to the office of* *Second Lieut.* *of Company D. Third Regiment* of the Militia of the State of Iowa, I, SAMUEL J. KIRKWOOD, Governor and Commander–in–Chief of the Militia of said State, in the name and by the authority of the people thereof, do commission him *Second Lieut* *of said Company* to take rank from the *31st* day of *May* *1861.* He is, therefore, carefully and diligently to discharge the duties of said office by doing and performing all manner of things, thereunto belonging: and I do strictly require all officers and soldiers under his command to be obedient to his orders, and he is to obey such orders and directions as he shall receive from time to time from his Commander–in–Chief, or his superior officer.

IN TESTIMONY WHEREOF, I have hereunto set my hand, and caused to be affixed the Great Seal of the State of Iowa.

Done at Des Moines, this *2nd* day of *June* in the year of our Lord, One Thousand Eight Hundred and Sixty of the Independence of the United States, the Eighty *fifth* and of this State, the *fifteenth.*

Samuel J. Kirkwood

BY THE GOVERNOR.

J. Bma Adjutant General.

Commission certificate for Lieutenant Ole Anderson

Ole suffered excruciating headaches because of that lead ball, headaches so severe they would block out everything else. He could not work. When he tried, sooner or later the bullet would move and he would flee, running from the pain.

He realized he had no future and he released Mary from her betrothal vow, told her to make a life without him. She would not hear of it. He needed her, she knew. She loved him and refused to leave him.

They married, lived on his pension and what she could earn as a seamstress.

There are newspaper stories about the Andersons, stories that tell of townsfolk grown accustomed to seeing Ole pacing the streets at night, striding through the town hour after hour until his need for sleep would overwhelm the pain in his head, or until Mary would find him and lead him home.

They are together now on a Decorah hillside cemetery, Mary and Ole and that musketball.

Another Ole Anderson

On the day the Wisconsin 15th left Madison, a 16 year old boy named Ole Anderson was walking from Waseca County, Minnesota, intending to join. Young Ole had persuaded his mother to let him go. He reached Madison three days late. The 15th was gone. Recruiters weren't sure what to do with the young Norwegian until one of them said, "Why don't we put him in the all-Irish 17th, no one can understand them either." The Irish spoke Celtic.

Young Ole's father, Andrew, enlisted five months later in the Minnesota 10th. It is unknown if the two ever met. Ole died of wounds near Atlanta in 1864; his father in a military hospital two years later.

Sigri Olsdatter Bergan

Sigri Olsdatter Bergan, from Numedal, Norway, married a man named Kristoffer Rugland. They had three sons, and then Kristoffer died.

Widow Sigri became engaged to marry again. Her fiancé went off to war. Sigri had his child. Word came back that her soldier had died.

So Sigri married a man named Ole Olson.

Her soldier fiancé survived and returned, too late to do anything about Sigri.

Sigri's story is in the Douglas County Historical Society library, but the soldier is not named.

John Bergh

Captain Robert Gordon said of one of his soldiers, "This man, John Bergh, a Norwegian by birth, has proven himself a good and true soldier. Has never been absent but once and then sick for five months after our miserable existence on the Yazoo River. He has been in all the battles and marches of the regiment and has never been known to falter or flinch in any occasion whatever."[1]

Ludvig Bjorn

Ludvig Bjorn, a pastor ordained in Norway, was newly arrived at a church in Manitowoc County, Wisconsin.

He enlisted and took 57 men from his congregation in with him. They became Company F of the all-Norwegian Wisconsin 15th.

Fourteen of his congregation of soldiers were wounded and two killed. Twelve were captured and sent to enemy prisons. Two died in Andersonville and one in Danville. Twelve died of disease and another nine were disabled.

Hans Christenson

Hans Christenson, from Brown County, Wisconsin, was sick during most of his first two years in the army. His record shows him going from one hospital to another.

Finally, he was healthy enough to be returned to his company, healthy enough to fight. In the battle of New Hope Church, he charged up Rocky Face Ridge and got killed, shot through his heart.

I Left St Loraner this
Morning at 6 OK and
came to Amherst at 9 am
and I camansed to work
for N Elsasman in the
Store Sowing and
Planting has comanst
all Over the conty
it as yet cole and no
green Grass up yet

SATURDAY 16

I Received a letter from
Capt Cook of Quincey
Lee in Relation to
a Boarding Bill with
I Cornoce and Capt
Cook Said in his letter
that such a bill was
Paid for more than a
yere ago to Mr
Adolph Sorenson
Provost Marshall of
Waupaca Co

SUNDAY 17

I want to Newhope
to Leutheran Church
and heard Rev Meekelsen
Pritching it was a
Large congregation out
and he don his Best
about Pritching but I
think that he himself
could Kry best of all
he don

I Recved a letter
from Capt Grinager
and he said that 44
Out of Our Regt have
Reinlisted and are
Expected to Madison this
Week I think it as som
what dautfull Whather
the are coming or Not as
I think them are tiend
of Soldiers life

TUESDAY 19

It Was a Scool Ex came
netions in Town of
Amherst to da and it
Was Mor Scool Mams Out
than you woued think
and all Wanted to get
Married I Recived
a letter from Miss
dated the Same day it
was Nothing New in
it all the folks was
Well

WEDNESDAY 20

I cant Write this morning
as I was up Cet Last
Night at Mr W s
and I come to the Store
at about 11 OK that Night
Mr H R Denny &
Mr Whilock was Over
heare to day an Mr H
R Denny Brought me
Over Two letters from

Excerpt from diary of
John Olson Wrolstad
describing Captain
Grinager's efforts to
recruit more men for the
Wisconsin 15th, especially
among veterans.

Ole Christoferson

Ole Christoferson, a 44 year old farmer in Kewaunee County, Wisconsin, was drafted, but did not report. There is a note in his military record stating that the Wisconsin 3rd Infantry Regiment paid $14.50 for Ole's arrest and delivery. The sheriff brought him in on October 31, 1864. Overnight he slipped away and they never did find him.

Mons Grinager

Mons Grinager, a farmer in Freeborn County, Minnesota, was commissioned a captain after enrolling and organizing Company K of the Wisconsin 15th. Many of his men were his neighbors around Albert Lea.

He was wounded at Stones River and was sent to a Union hospital at Murfreesboro, Tennessee, which was overrun by Confederate forces. Grinager had been a prisoner for five days when reinforced Northern troops threatened to retake the hospital. He hid by crawling into an under-stairway closet and avoided being taken away with the other prisoners.

Kittel Halvorsen

Kittel Halvorsen of Winchester, Wisconsin, was born Kittel Halvorsen Kjeldahl in the Hjartdal commune of Telemark in the village of Tuddal. He was wounded at Mission Ridge.

After the war he settled near Belgrade in Stearns County, Minnesota. He was elected to the Minnesota legislature in 1885 and to the U.S. Congress in 1890.

Knud Hanson

Knud Hanson, from Winchester, Wisconsin, was drafted into the Wisconsin First Cavalry, Company F, on November 24, 1863. He was captured on July 30, 1864, and died in Andersonville prison on April 28, 1865. He is in grave 12,848.

He is the last identified prisoner to die there; two "unknowns" were buried later that day.

Captain Mons Grinager, Wisconisin 15th Infantry, Company K

Carl Helgeson

Carl Helgeson, age 19, enlisted from Eau Claire in the Wisconsin First Cavalry. Nothing special about him other than that, after the war, he married a girl from Colfax, Wisconsin, named Sigvi Severtsen and they moved to Montevideo, Minnesota, and they had four children.

Then one morning Helgeson and a neighbor girl took off together and went to Nebraska. Carl Helgeson changed his name to Charley Johnson. And they had five children.

Jens S. Jensen

Jens S. Jensen came with his parents and six siblings to Bosque County, Texas, in 1853. He was drafted into the Confederate Army and assigned to McCord's Frontier Regiment of Texas Cavalry. He served four years.

Jensen's grandson, Maury Jensen, who lives in Stillwater, Minnesota, tells a family story that after the South surrendered, Private Jens Jensen went back to his home in Clifton and somewhere on his farm he buried his guns. They've never been found.

Osmund Johnson and the Wedding Ghost

Osmund Johnson and his bride, Barbro, came from Rogaland in 1858. They made their way to Fillmore County, Minnesota, where they got a little farm.

Then came the Civil War. A recruiter from Wisconsin told Osmund about a new regiment being organized in Madison, an infantry regiment in which all the officers and men would be like him, Norwegians. Johnson signed his name, and went off to fight for his new country. He left Barbro to operate their small farm, after arranging with the Norwegian bachelor on the next farm to help her.

Private Johnson served in several battles, and all went well until a September day in 1863. His company battled Confederate forces at Chickamauga, Georgia. Johnson advanced through heavy gunfire. He fell, shot in the back of his head. Word came back to Minnesota that Barbro was a widow.

Two years went by, and she found herself courted by the helpful farmer next door. She accepted, and began preparing for their wedding. The blessed day came, and with it a surprise – a soldier, so emaciated he needed help to stand, so thin no uniform was small enough, insisting that he was Osmund, that he was her husband.

Barbro, it is said, did not recognize him, refused to believe him. This skeleton, this hollow-eyed joker, could not be the man she had sent away, could not be the man she had so grieved over. That man was gone, long dead, and buried God knows where.

But the soldier persisted, telling his story. Almost dead on that battlefield, he was picked up by Confederates, sent to a prison hospital in Danville, Virginia, and from there to Andersonville prison in Georgia, where starvation and scurvy put him in that prison's hospital. It was not a place to get well. The Andersonville prison hospital was, for most, a brief stop on one's way to the burial ditch. But

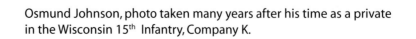

Osmund Johnson, photo taken many years after his time as a private in the Wisconsin 15th Infantry, Company K.

Osmund hung on and refused to give up. He made it through, survived in Andersonville longer than any other prisoner, and here he was.

Barbro finally accepted that he was who he claimed to be. She took him home, fed him good food, nursed him back to health. The neighbor remained their good friend and they shared many years, it is said, she happily with the man she married and the man she almost married.

Ole Julson

Forty-year-old Ole Julson from Waterloo, Grant County, Wisconsin, was in Company H of the Wisconsin 50th Infantry. His unit was on the steamer *Post Boy* on the Missouri River. Somehow, Private Ole got into an argument with his company commander, Captain Charles Cox.

The muster roll states that Ole shot and killed his captain and then jumped overboard, and was believed to have drowned.

Gunder Killor

Gunder Killor from Wanamingo, Minnesota, was drafted into the Minnesota 10th Infantry. What would a man named Killor do in a war? He ran away.

Knud Knudsen

"I got a bullet in my right arm and one through the calf of my left leg, and I have one in my back just under the shoulder blade, which has grown in, and one in my hip which has grown in, and another through my hip which came out again, and one I got in my right side and the bullet came out through my stomach on the upper side of the navel."[2]

Knud Knudsen wrote those words in a letter sent to his family and friends back in Stjernes, Rollag, Numedahl, Norway. He told of being in the battle of Stones River, Tennessee, on New Years Eve, 1862.

In five months, Private Knudsen was out of the hospital and on his way back to his company, three of the bullets still in him. A newspaper in Norway, telling his story, said it was obvious the South was going to lose America's Civil War, since it had to spend so many bullets on one Union soldier, and even then failed to do away with him.

Stark Larson

Private Stark Larson, 15th Wisconsin Infantry, Company B, disappeared from the train that was carrying his regiment from Chicago to Alton, Illinois. He had gone out on the platform of the car in which he had been riding and had fallen off. It was assumed he had been killed. But a few months later he showed up, rejoining his company at Mississippi River Island No. 10.

Hendrik Larsen Lien

Not all young Norwegians were willing to enlist. Hendrik Larsen Lien from Hallingdal, Norway, came to America in 1845 and settled near East Koshkonong, Wisconsin. He was drafted and bought his way out. Sold his prize team of colts and used the money to hire a substitute.

Christian Lund

Christian Lund from Farsund, Norway, sailed to America, landed at New Orleans and was pressed into service in the Confederate army. He ran away and made his way through the lines to the North and enlisted in the Union army. He fought at Fort Donelson and at Vicksburg, and was wounded. He rose through the ranks to become a captain.

After the war, Lund went to Duluth, Minnesota, and became a sailing master on the Great Lakes.

Hans Nelson

Private Hans Nelson of Decorah, Iowa, told of fighting near Vicksburg and of talking with the enemy, shouting across to them one evening. The Confederates belonged to two Missouri regiments that Nelson's unit had met in three previous battles.

Nelson wrote that some of the enemy came over and stacked their arms and the soldiers, North and South, talked for a long time. "Our men cooked coffee and treated them," Nelson said later, "and when they had talked together as long as they cared to, each one took up his position again and they began to fire at each other again, but," Nelson added, "not as hard as before."

The next night, he said, nine of the Missouri soldiers came over and surrendered. After that some came every night, saying their food was running out.

Nelson ended his letter "Greet the girls for me, first those whom I know and after that, all of the rest of them."[3]

Knute Nelson

Knute Nelson came to America at age seven. He and his mother arrived at Castle Garden, New York City, on July 4, 1849, to find Americans celebrating their national day with fireworks and parades.

Knute's mother had no money, and had to beg from another passenger to pay the disembarkation fee. There is a story that young Knute comforted his fearful, weeping mother by saying "Don't cry, Mother, we are poor now, but when I get big, I shall stand next to the King."

Knute, in 1861, enlisted in the Wisconsin 4th Infantry, Company B. He was 18. He was taken prisoner in a charge on breastworks at Port Hudson. He and three comrades had advanced to within 20 yards of the breastworks when they were hit. One of the Union men was killed, another wounded mortally, a third unhurt, and Knute wounded in a thigh by a piece of shrapnel that was never removed.

After Port Hudson surrendered, Knute found himself back in his own company. He was promoted to corporal. He was discharged on July 14, 1864.

Knute Nelson, photo taken after the war when he served as a U.S. senator.

After the war, Nelson married Nicholina Jacobson, an immigrant from Toten, and began a lifelong interest in politics. He studied law and he served two terms in the Wisconsin legislature. In 1871, he moved his family to Alexandria, Minnesota. He was elected to the United States Congress in 1882 and served three terms. He was elected Governor of Minnesota in 1892. He became a United States Senator and served five terms, from 1895 to 1923.

'Carl' Olson

The *Chicago Hemlandet* in its July 17, 1861, issue used the word "pretty" in describing 'Carl' Olson. It took the Regiment three weeks to discover that 'Carl' was Caroline. Her father was sent for. He came and took her home. She was soon back, hair cut short, wearing boy's clothes, going unit to unit, trying to enlist. The paper reported that she got into the Illinois 19th, Company F, for awhile, but her name is not on their muster rolls.

Ebrah Olson

Ebrah Olson, 18, was from Preston, Wisconsin. His unit, the Wisconsin 30th Infantry, had been ordered to New Lisbon, Wisconsin, on September 10, 1863, to put down a draft riot. One of the rioters, firing a revolver, shot Olson through his chest. He's buried in Madison.

Sven Olson

Sven Olson landed at New Orleans in 1846 along with his wife and infant child, his father and some others, hoping to go to Texas. The other families moved on, but Sven could not afford to hire a wagon. So he got a large log and made himself a wheelbarrow. He pushed it, while his wife, Asborg, walked beside him, carrying their child. Eventually, they reached Brownsboro, Texas.

Sven enlisted in a Texas unit and saw action at Vicksburg and at Shiloh. He survived the war; lived to age 84.

Henry Peterson

Henry Peterson, from Winchester, Wisconsin, enlisted in the Wisconsin 11th, Company K.   Records list him as 18 years old, but he lied about his age. He was actually 15 and may have been the youngest infantry rifleman in the war.

There is a family story that his future bride, Anne Twito, first saw him as he and other returning soldiers were disembarking from a river steamer at Brownsville, Minnesota. Henry and Anne married and had six children. They farmed awhile near Highlandville, on the Iowa-Minnesota border, and then moved to Lake Mills, Iowa.

Henry often worked for other farmers and, after gathering his day's pay, would stop at a tavern to wash the dust from his throat. He often stayed late. Some nights he forgot to come home.

And then he didn't come home at all. After 27 years, Anne Peterson, certain that by now Henry was dead, filed for a widow's pension.

The pension board turned her down, saying it was already paying a pension to her husband and they gave his address in Portland, Oregon.

Anne Peterson and a son-in-law traveled west and found Henry living with a second wife. Mother and son-in-law came back to Iowa, and some weeks later Henry's western wife, distraught over finding she had been married so many years to a bigamist with six children, hanged herself.

George Anderson Linnevold,
Iowa 38th Infantry, Company E

Eventually Henry returned to Lake Mills and, so a family story tells, he and Anne had a long talk, during which he promised to quit drinking. She offered to take him back, and both agreed neither would ever again talk about his 27-year absence. And they didn't. They lived together for another 15 years, quite happily it seems, because Anne was once heard to say she finally had the husband she always wanted.

John Peterson

John Peterson of Keokuk, Iowa, joined the Iowa 37th. He was 45, minimum age in the 37th. That unit was called the "Silver Grays" – average age 53, eldest 80, a man from Muscatine named Curtis King.

The 37th was never sent into battle; it was assigned to guard railroads around St. Louis, the prison at Alton, Illinois, supply trains near Memphis and prisoners in Ohio.

The men served their three years and were mustered out in May 1865.

Two Unidentified Soldiers

A Norwegian soldier named Jorgen – perhaps George Anderson (Linnevold) – told of marching through a southern town. He said the people had never seen a Yankee soldier and had the idea that Yankee soldiers murdered and plundered wherever they went. He told of spending a night at a house where a little girl said she had always heard that Yankee soldiers had hooves and tails.[4]

A Norwegian soldier, writing to his family, said "Every night we lie with our rifles on our arms. We think we shall be fighting in a few days. If I die my grave will be here in Missouri."[5]

[1] Robert Gordon, Captain, Company K, 25th Wisconsin, transcribed in *Red Book*, vol. 30. The *Red Book* is the popular name for *Series 1144 Regimental and Descriptive Rolls*, a series of books, one for each military unit, containing information copied in 1866 from the *Series 1200* records.

[2] Letter printed in *Stavanger amtstidene og adresseavig*, December 14, 1863, quoted in Theodore C. Blegen, *Norwegian Migration to America*, vol. 2, Norwegian-American Historical Association, 1940, p.398.

[3] Letter dated June 20, 1863, from a typed translation in the Vesterheim Norwegian-American Museum Archive.

[4] Transcription of a letter in the Vesterheim Norwegian-American Museum Archive, Linnevold Collection.

[5] From a typed translation in the Vesterheim Norwegian-American Museum Archive.

War Digest

[Handwritten letter in Norwegian, partially legible]

St. Louis Oct. 31st /65

Kjær Ven Nils

Din Meget kjærkomne Skrivelse imodtog
Jeg for Nogle dage Siden for hvilken
Jeg Skjælder dig Men Størst Tak for. Jeg
Saa der I te Men Stor glæd I di alle
havde kilen Sam Jeg og Sad hav af Jeads
Naald berete dig Jeu vi har vist Start
t tek den ... gudfar Sam giver ...
Senhed og helbred Men Jeg kan vist betlage
for Min del I Jeg Sjønes Saa lidet der Tan
Jeg Sad I En Skrivelse ifra Min ...
I Naar lile Sen var Syge Men Jeg har
Ikke hørt Noget ifra dem Siden og ...
En till Sielen Jeg havde Brev ifra
... Jeg vil ikke var Sand Mankene Enten
... Ikke har till at Skrive Nu siden

According to Frances H. Kennedy, in *The Civil War Battlefield Guide*, published in 1990, the number of soldiers who died in the Civil War, both Union and Confederate, has been set at 624,511, of whom 388,580 (62%) died of disease. Leading causes, in decreasing numbers, were: diarrhea; typhoid, typhus and malarial fevers; pneumonia; measles.

Battle deaths: North, 110,000; South, 94,000.

There were 194,000 Union troops in Confederate prisons and about 30,000 (15%) died. There were 214,000 Confederate troops in Union prisons and about 26,000 (12%) died.

Forty percent of the men in the Union army were 21 and under.

Union privates were paid $13 a month until May 1864, $16 a month after that.

Black troops were paid $10 a month. There were 178,975 black troops enrolled.

The Military Draft began April 16, 1862 in the South; March 3, 1863 in the North.

Civil War Infantry Song

Lincoln rides a gray horse,
Davis rides a mule.
Lincoln is a gentleman,
Jeff Davis is a fool.

A pint of meal, ground cobs and all,
Was served to every man;
For want of fire we ate it raw
In Dixie's sunny land.

– Florence Heineck Spors, Onalaska, Wis.

Left and opposite page: Two letters written by Private Sjur Sjursen of the Wisconsin 49th Infantry. Letters from soldiers were not censored by the army and often provide personal descriptions of their experiences.

All hail, Norsemen, descendants of the Vikings, let your hordes, as in days of old, sweep down upon the South, crushing as with Tor's hammer the Southerner who meets you on the field of battle.

> –The final line of a recruitment report issued by the United States army, quoted in Waldemar Ager, *Colonel Heg and His Boys*, Norwegian-American Historical Association, 2000, p.xv.

Bounties

A federal enlistment bounty (bonus) of $100 began in 1861; $300 for a three year term was begun in October 1863. States soon began adding to that, most as much as $100. In New York State, the cavalry advertised $777 for officers, $677 for all others. Counties added more. The War Board in Winneshiek County, Iowa, voted to pay a bounty of $50. Towns added more, $10 to the enlistee, and a promise to give $8 a month to the soldier's wife and $4 to each child, pledging to take care of them should the soldier fail to return.

In October, 1864, to avoid having to draft men, the city of Madison, Wisconsin, began adding $200 to the enlistment bounty. Other towns soon followed.

The federal bounty for veterans reenlisting was $402. Persons bringing in such a veteran were paid $25.

Only a portion of this bounty money was paid at the time of muster. A soldier enlisting for $300 could get a maximum of $60 then and $60 every six months after that. Many, including most Norwegian soldiers, chose to take as little each time as they could, saving the greater amount for their discharge. That, together with the usual muster-out money of $50, plus warrants for land (160 acres), gave them farms with money enough for buildings, livestock and equipment.

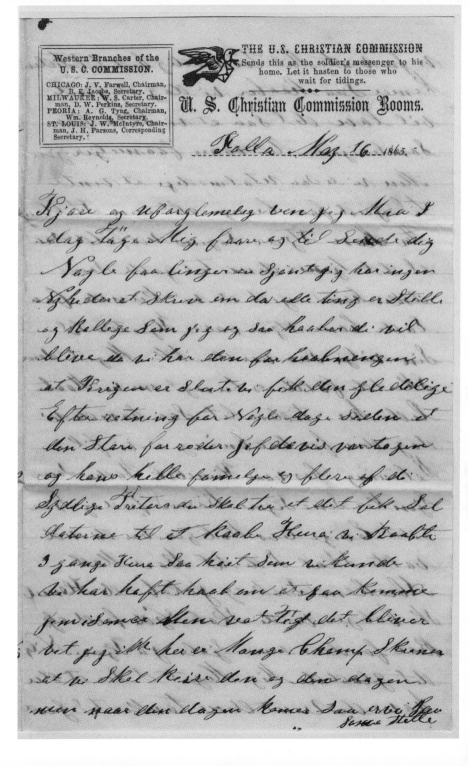

All the Negroes run away from their masters and come to our camp where they can be safe and are beyond the reach of the cat-o'-nine-tails. They are very happy because we came to free them from their cruel slavery.

> – Thomas Emmonson in a letter to his brother, Albert, written on May 15, 1862 from Mississippi River Island No. 10, quoted in Waldemar Ager, *Colonel Heg and His Boys*, Norwegian-American Historical Association, 2000, p.123.

We were immediately ordered into formation, and charged the earthworks with fixed bayonets and shrill hurrahs and other noise and yelling, more like the shrieking of pigs than anything else. This business of making such a terrible noise is a peculiar characteristic of the Irish. We made short work, and our losses were small. The enemy fled when he saw that his resistance was in vain. We took more than thirteen hundred prisoners that day. There were many dead and wounded.

> – An unidentified Norwegian soldier, whose letter, written from Newport News, Virginia, on March 31, 1862, was found in the files of the Norwegian newspaper *Morgenbladet* (Oslo) dated July 24, 1862. The letter is in Brynjolf J. Hovde, "Three Civil War Letters from 1862," *Studies and Records of the Norwegian–American Historical Association*, vol. IV, 1929, p. 78.

Muster roll for the Illinois 82nd Infantry, Company I, listing the articles of clothing each man received.

Provision Return for Captain _Isaac P. Kerr_ Company _C, 1st_ _Va_ Regiment of _Cavalry_ for _Three_ days, commencing _28th_ day of _Jun_ 186_2_, and ending _30th_ day of _Jun_ 186_2_.

POST OR STATION	Number of men	Number of women	TOTAL	Number of days	Number of rations	Pork	Salt Beef	Fresh Beef	Bacon	Hard Bread	Flour	Peas	Rice	Coffee	Tea	Sugar	Vinegar	Sperm	Adamantine	Tallow	Soap	Salt	Dessic'd Potatoes	Mixed Vegetables	Soft Bread	REMARKS
																RATIONS OF			Candles							
New Creek	56		56	3	168	48			120	120	48	168		168		168	168	168			168	168				

Isaac P. Kerr ____ Commanding Company.

The A. C. S. will issue agreeable to the above return.

Henry Anisansel Col ____ Commanding Post.

Provisions record, listing the food rations for 56 men for three days.

The battle was fought on the thirty-first of May and the first of June. On the first day we were beaten back, and seventeen cannon had to be left behind to fall into enemy hands. They could not be carried along, as nearly all the horses had been shot. Fifteen thousand of our troops were forced to run away from their camp leaving behind their standing tents and their knapsacks, which, however, gave the enemy little comfort; he was compelled to leave it all again the next morning, because we had received reinforcements during the night, and our soldiers drove the enemy out at the point of the bayonet. All the knapsacks belonging to our soldiers had been cut open, and all that our enemies could use had been taken out, for they are poorly clad and as a rule they have only a pair of trousers and a gray cap. But they fight very well, nevertheless, because they are fed with all sorts of fables and fine promises. Money they do not get, for that sort of thing is a luxury with them... except paper money, which they are forced to accept. However, when parts of their territory are taken by our troops, then their money becomes mere waste paper.

> – An unidentified Norwegian soldier whose letter, written from Richmond, Virginia, on June 19, 1862, was found in the files of the Norwegian newspaper *Morgenbladet* (Oslo) dated July 24, 1862. The letter is in Brynjolf J. Hovde, "Three Civil War Letters from 1862," Studies and Records of the Norwegian–American Historical Association, vol. IV, 1929, p. 88.

Two boys from our regiment drank from a bottle which they thought contained whisky. They became so sick that we had to take them to the hospital. There both died within a few hours. I regret that I remember neither their names nor the company to which they belonged.

> – Bersven Nelson, Wisconsin 15th Inf. Co. I. Residence: Elk Mound, Eau Claire County, Wisconsin. In "Notes of a Civil War Soldier," Norwegian-American Studies, vol. 26, Norwegian-American Historical Association, 1974, p. 127.

We left Decorah the 30th of June and we traveled along the Mississippi for 300 miles and came to a town called Clinton at 2 o'clock in the afternoon. In the evening every man got a blanket and in the morning we got our clothes. We put up our tents, 16 men in each tent. We got cooking and eating utensils and everything we are supposed to have here. I am well and strong and of good courage. We have good officers and the work is not hard. We drill three hours a day. I have heard them say there are 986 men in this place. When the regiment is filled we shall go to Washington. They say we will get paid in a few days. When I get my pay I will send you something to remember me by.

> – Jens Johannesen, a soldier from Fillmore County, Minnesota, unit undetermined, writing to his mother on August 1, 1862, from a typed translation in the Vesterheim Norwegian-American Museum Archive.

There was fighting 27 miles from Springfield...Our battery set out for there in the morning and the next morning they were on the place. There were about 6,100 Rebels there and 15,000 of our men. The battle was at a small town. Our men fell back as they wished to get the enemy into the town. When they had done so, our battery fired on them. The Rebels thought they could protect themselves by being in between the houses. We threw bombs and bullets into the houses and in all 1700 men died in the city, and we took many prisoners. They say the Rebels fear to go so near us again.

- Jens Johannessen, Iowa 18th Infantry, Company A, in a letter written to his family on September 20, 1862, from a typed translation in the Vesterheim Norwegian-American Museum Archive.

By noon we came to a little town. There we found four saddled horses which belonged to the marauders, but the owners were nowhere to be seen. We then made an about-face and started for our camp. We had not gone far before a mounted man in civilian dress caught up with us and presented himself as a farmer. Our captain, however, and others among us were not satisfied with this explanation. The man was searched. We found some papers in his possession that proved he was a courier for General Forrest, who was in command of a part of the Confederate cavalry and had orders to inflict all the damage possible on the Union forces along the Mississippi. We took the courier captive and shipped him up to Columbus, where he was grilled by a court martial and found guilty of treason as the leader of a band of bushwhackers. We never did learn whether he was hung, which he probably deserved to be.

- Bersven Nelson, Wisconsin 15th Inf. Co. I. Residence: Elk Mound, Eau Claire County, Wisconsin. In "Notes of a Civil War Soldier," Norwegian-American Studies, vol. 26, Norwegian-American Historical Association, 1974, pp.136-7.

See how we live: on the one hand, the prospect of being carried off as cannon fodder to the South; on the other, the imminent danger of falling prey to the Indians; add to this the heavy war tax and everybody has to pay whether he is enlisted as a soldier or not. You are better off who can live at home in peaceful Norway. God grant us patience and fortitude to bear these heavy burdens.

- An anonymous letter from a Norwegian immigrant in Dodge County, Minnesota, that appeared in *Morgenbladet*, a newspaper in Norway, on November 22, 1862.

The Civil War Draft

The draft was enacted by Congress in March 1863.

All white men, ages 20 to 45, who were citizens, plus aliens of those ages who have declared their intention to naturalize, were required to register. Married men 20 to 35, and unmarried men 20 to 45, unless physically disabled, had to serve if called.

Young men, 17 to 19, could serve with permission from parent or guardian.

We fished two cannon out of the river, which the rebels had sunk when they left the Island. They were twelve-pounders, i.e, designed to fire balls weighing 12 pounds. We cleaned and polished them until they looked really good. But as we did not have the right kind of balls, we could not use them.

> – Bersven Nelson, Wisconsin 15th Inf. Co. I. Residence: Elk Mound, Eau Claire County, Wisconsin. In "Notes of a Civil War Soldier," *Norwegian-American Studies*, vol. 26, Norwegian-American Historical Association, 1974, p. 143.

One more in our regiment was killed. He was Norwegian. His name was Bendik Bendiksen and he lived in the neighborhood of Calmar. He belonged to Co. D. He was the first in our regiment to become a victim of the bullets of the enemy.

> – George M. Anderson, 2nd Brigade, Iowa 38th Regiment, Co. E., writing to his parents and siblings from a camp near Vicksburg on June 19, 1863, from a transcription in the Vesterheim Norwegian-American Archive, Linnevold Collection.

This morning I was up and watched them fire the large cannons, and I saw a ball take one of the enemy's flags off the fort. Immediately someone came and tried to put it up again but a rifle bullet took him and the flag away and immediately another one came but he was given the same treatment and then they gave up. I saw no more men try it.

> – Hans A. Nelson, Iowa 3rd Regiment, Co. D, writing to a friend from a camp near Vicksburg on June 20, 1863, from a typed translation in the Vesterheim Norwegian-American Museum Archive.

According to E. B. Quiner in *The Military History of Wisconsin in the War for the Union*, published in 1866, after June, 1863, soldiers who were at least nine months into their first enlistments were urged to reenlist for three years. This enabled them to qualify for veteran reenlistment bonuses of $402 and to become eligible for 30-day furloughs. The furlough usually began at the time of the reenlistment, but could be delayed. It had to be granted sometime before expiration of the soldier's initial enlistment period.

I had a bullet hole shot through my hat, which caused no pain; but then I was taken prisoner – and that was something that did pain me.

> – Ole Steensland, describing his role in the battle of Chickamauga, Georgia, quoted in Waldemar Ager, Colonel Heg and His Boys, Norwegian-American Historical Association, 2000, p.148.

It is frightfully hot today. We are keeping ourselves in some holes which we have dug in the ground to protect ourselves from the rebel sharpshooters. But it is so hot in these holes that it almost kills us.

> – Morten J. Nordre, from a letter dated June 28, 1864, quoted in Blegen, p. 398.

One day's ration consisted of two shares of half rotten meat, half a loaf of bread and something that was called soup – it consisted primarily of lukewarm water and half-cooked black beans, best known by the name Negro beans. Each man got from a quarter to half a pot. In a pot of this soup one could sometimes find two dozen beans; at other times, it was completely impossible to find even one.

> – Anthon Odin Øyen, in a letter written February 14, 1866, telling of the food at Libby Prison, Richmond, Virginia.

According to the Adjutant General's Office, Washington, D.C., May 30, 1865, on muster out, men who had been prisoners of war were given three months additional pay.

Private Ole Steensland, Wisconsin 15th Infantry, Company E

Names

Anyone searching Norwegian soldiers is handicapped by changing names.
Young Norwegians used one name in Norway, frequently another in the army and a third after the war was over.

In Norway a young man would be known by his given name and his father's. As an example, Ole, son of Johan, would be known as Ole Johansen. If additional identity was needed, he would add his farm name, Myre; he was Ole Johansen who lived on Myre.

When he came to America and enlisted, he gave his name as he generally did "Ole Johansen" and the Yankee clerk would write "Ole Johnson" and "Ole Johnson" is how the soldier would be known.

An additional point of confusion results from the fact that Norway was a part of Sweden in the nineteenth century. An enlistee might give his place of birth as Norway; the Yankee clerk would write Sweden.

After the war, the immigrant soldier acquired a farm, got married, started a family and began to think seriously about what he wanted himself and his farm to be called. Take, for example, Sergeant George Johnson of the Wisconsin 15th, Company G. He came to America in 1854. After the war, he acquired a farm near Ridgeway, Winneshiek County, Iowa. He took back his baptismal name, adopted his old Norway farm name, and became Guttorm Hovden. It took help from Guttorm Hovden's grandchildren to connect their grandfather to soldier George Johnson.

A majority of young Norwegians enlisting in the Union army are known in the military records by their patronyms, their given names plus their father's, adding "sen" or "son." Very often their descendants do not know these soldiers by the names they used in the Army, but instead by names used after the war, and it takes a lot of searching to connect the two.

Ole Hanson of Winneshiek County, Iowa, came to America in 1862 and joined the Iowa 13th Regiment, Company G. He is known for the diaries he kept, both before and during the war. Vesterheim has them; museum visitors can hear a voice reading a portion of one telling about his arrival. Soldier Ole Hanson after the war became O. H. Nass.

Jorgen Andersen immigrated from Lier, Norway. His Winneshiek County, Iowa, neighbors knew him as George Linnevold.

Norwegians in America's Wars

Names of Norwegian soldiers were spelled in the American military records in the following ways:

Aaker	Aker	Christianson	Christensen, Christenson, Christiansen, Crestensen
Abrahamson	Abramson	Christopherson	Christerferson, Christofasen, Christofferson, Christophersen
Amundson	Ammendson, Ammison, Ammondson, Ammunnson, Amondsen, Amondson, Amonson, Amunson, Amundsen, Armonsen, Emenson	Dahl	Dal, Dall, Doll
		Eide	Heide
Anundson	Annenson, Annunsen, Anonsen, Anunsen, Anunson, Anuson	Ellickson	Alackson, Alaksen, Aleckson, Allexson, Elicson, Elikson
Anderson	Andresen, Enderson, Enersen	Ellison	Allison, Elleson
Arneson	Arnison	Ellefson	Elefson, Ellafson, Ellefsen, Ellison
Bendickson	Bendicksen, Bendixon	Engebretson	Engbertson, Engebertsen, Engebertson, Engebretsen, Engebrigtsen, Ingbretson, Ingebretsen, Ingebretson, Ingebrigtsen, Inglebretsen, Inglebritson
Benson	Bendsen		
Bjornson	Bairnson, Bohnson, Asbjornson		
Bolstad	Baalstad	Erickson	Arrickson, Earicson, Erekson, Ericksen, Eriksen, Erikson, Erixson, Errickson
Borstad	Borstaad		
		Everson	Evertson, Ivarson, Iverson
Brown	Bruhn, Brun		

Gilbertson	Gilberson, Gilbrandson, Gulbranson, Gulbrandsen, Gulbranson, Gulbronson, Guldbrenson
Gullickson	Golaxon, Gulickson, Gullicksen, Gullikson, Gullixson
Gunderson	Gunnerson, Gunnesen
Haakenson	Haagensen, Haakinsen, Haakenson, Hoakinson, Hogensen, Hogenson, Hogonson, Hokanson
Halvorson	Alverson, Halversen, Halvorsen, Halvurson, Holverson, Hulverson
Hanson	Hansan, Hansson
Henrikson	Hendrickson, Hendrikson, Henricksen, Henrickson
Holland	Haaland, Halland, Helland, Holand, Hollan
Hovland	Hofland, Hoveland
Isaacson	Isaacsen, Isaacsen, Isaakson, Isackson, Isaksen, Izackson
Jacobson	Jakobson, Jokomsen, Jokumson
Jamison	Jameson, Jemison, Jemson
Jansen	Janssen
Johanson	Johanesen, Johaneson, Johannesen, Johanneson, Johannessen, Johansen,
Johnson	Jahnsan, Joanson, Jonson, Johnston
Jorginsen	Jargenson, Jarginson, Jergenson, Jergeson, Jorganson, Jorgenson, Jurgenson
Knudson	Canuteson, Kanudson, Kenutzen, Kneudson, Knudsen, Knudtson, Knuteson, Knutsen, Knutson, Neutson
Kolbe	Colby
Larson	Larcen, Larsen
Lawson	Lassen, Lasseson
Louison	Lewison, Liosen
Mathison	Matheisen, Mathewson, Mathiasen, Mathiasson, Mathiesen, Mathisen, Matsen, Matson, Matthiesen, Mattison, Mattson
Mickelson	Mekelson, Michelsen, Michelson, Mickelsen, Mikkelsen, Mikkelson
Monson	Monsen, Munsen, Munson

Nelson	Neilsen, Neilson, Nielsen, Nielson, Nilsen, Nilson	Torkelson	Torkelsen, Torkildsen, Torkilson, Torgleson
Olson	Ohlson, Oldson, Oldston, Olesen, Oleson, Olsen, Olssen, Olsson, Osolsson	Torstenson	Torstensen, Torstenston, Tostenson
Osmundson	Aasmundsen		
Ostenson	Aastensen		
Peterson	Patterson, Pedersen, Pederson, Petersen		
Reierson	Reiersen, Ryersen		
Seim	Saim, Sime		
Severson	Seversen, Sivertsen, Siverson, Syversen, Syverson		
Simonson	Simonsen		
Swenson	Svendsen, Svendson, Svensen, Swanson, Swinson		
Thompson	Thomason, Thomassen		
Thoreson	Thoresen, Thorsen, Thorson		
Torgerson	Tergerson, Torgersen, Torgison, Torgusen, Torguson		

Database Entries

A database of over 10,000 Norwegians who fought in the Civil War is available at Vesterheim's website, <www.vesterheim.org>. The following are entries from that database for some of the soldiers mentioned in this book.

AKER, Lars Knudsen MN 3rd Inf. Co. D. Residence: Red Wing, Goodhue County, Minnesota. Born 19 Sep. 1825 in Lærdal, Telemark, Norway, the son of Knud Saavesen Aaker and Mari Larsdatter Haegtvedt. Came to America with his parents at age 20. Settled in Dane County, Wisconsin. Married Kathrine Helvig Westrem of Graven Parish, Hardanger, at East Koshkonong Church on 13 Feb. 1853. Three children. Moved to Goodhue County, Minnesota, in 1857. Elected to the Minnesota Legislature; he resigned his seat to accept, on 4 Oct. 1861, a commission as a first lieutenant. Civil War: Age 36. Mustered 10 Oct. 1861. Resigned his commission on 30 Mar. 1862 because of ill health. Moved to Alexandria, Minnesota. His wife died 25 Feb. 1879. Married Karen Celisa Akre of Karmoen Island on 23 Aug. 1882. Four children. In 1884, they moved to Crookston, Minnesota. He died in Crookston in 1895. Sources: (MCIW p.184) (MINN p.119, 136) (O. N. Nelson, *History of the Scandinavians in the United States*, Minneapolis, 1893. p.315) (*America-America Letters*, Norwegian-American Historical Association, 2001, p. xxi, pp. 105-157, photo p.106) (ULVESTAD p.256) "Akers, Lars" "Aaker, Lars"

ANDERSON, Andrew MN 10th Inf. Co. E. Residence: Manchester, Freeborn County, Minnesota. Born in Bragernes, Buskerud, Norway, 27 Jan. 1820. Came to America, to Milwaukee, Wisconsin, in October 1853, and to Freeborn County, Minnesota, in 1857. Wife was Gloria Olson of Hartland, in Freeborn County. Their teenage son, Ole, had enlisted earlier in 1862. Civil War: Age 43. Enrolled 18 Aug. 1862. Mustered 13 Oct. 1862. Private. Discharged from the service 20 May 1865, absent from his unit at time of discharge. Apparently he was in a hospital. He died 5 Nov. 1866, weakened, it was said, by the "severe life and many hardships endured in the army." Buried in Bancroft Central church cemetery. Andrew Anderson's tombstone shows birth as 13 Dec. 1819. Sources: (MINN p.474) (MCIW p.479) (FCHS) (Letter, Alan Anderson, Mercer Island, Washington)

ANDERSON, George IA 38th Inf. Co. E. Residence: Frankville Township, seven miles southeast of Decorah, Winneshiek County, Iowa. Was living there in 1853. Born "Jorgen Andersen" at Lier, Drammen, Norway. Civil War: Age 26. Enlisted 15 Aug. 1862 as corporal. Mustered 4 Nov. 1862. Transferred to Iowa 34th and 38th Infantry Consolidated Co. K on 1 Jan. 1865. Promoted to sergeant. Mustered out 15 Aug. 1865, Houston, Texas. After the war, took name "Linnevold, Jorgen." Buried at Washington Prairie Lutheran Church Cemetery, Decorah, Iowa. Stone reads "George M. Linnevold, Jan. 5, 1836 – Mar. 1, 1925, IA 38th Inf. Co. E, 1861-1865." Sources: (ISW-V p.407, 846) (ULVESTAD p.260) (DGA) (Willard Linnevold, Decorah, Iowa) (KJR) (Wisconsin Cemetery Records) (HEDBERG) "Linnevold, George M."

ANDERSON, Ole WI 17th Inf. Co. D. Residence: Manchester, Freeborn County, Minnesota. Born 10 Aug. 1846 at Lier, Buskerud, Norway, a son of Andrew Anderson, who enlisted in the Minnesota 10th Infantry. Civil War: Age 15. Said to have walked from Waseca County, Minnesota, to Madison, Wisconsin, to enlist in the all-Norwegian 15th Infantry. That unit had already left Madison when Ole arrived, so he joined the 17th, an all-Irish regiment. Enlisted for three years on 5 Mar. 1862 at Madison. Mustered there the same day. Private. Wounded in the Battle for Atlanta, Georgia, on 2 Aug. 1864 and died of his wounds eight days later. Buried in the National Cemetery at Atlanta. Sources: (SHSW *Red Book*, vol. 22, p.28) (LOVE p.1086) (QUINER p. 653) (Letter, Alan Anderson, Mercer Island, Washington) (Clipping from *The Waseca Minnesota Journal*, undated) (FCHS – History of Freeborn County p. 715)

ANDERSON, Ole A. IA 3rd Inf. Co. D. Residence: Decorah, Winneshiek County, Iowa. Born 21 Oct. 1833 in Vestre Slidre, Valders, Norway. Came to America in 1850. Civil War: Age 28. Enlisted 21 May 1861 as second lieutenant. Mustered 8 June 1861. Wounded in head dangerously 17 Sep. 1861, at Blue Mills, Missouri. Shot in the left temple, ball remained in his head the rest of his life. Discharged from the service 16 Aug. 1862 on account of wounds. Ole A. Anderson was granted a pension of $50 a month because of the gunshot wound to his head. On 17 Sep. 1862 he married Mary Hanson Katterud. In 1885, Ole A. Anderson was living in Decorah, Iowa, at 407 East Water Street. He died 29 Jan. 1910 and was buried in Decorah Lutheran Cemetery, 50 yards inside Cemetery Drive gate, left side, near road; stone shows dates "1833-1910." Sources: (ISW-I p.297) (XSS Iowa p.235) (Pension List, 1882-3; vol. 3, p. 813) (ULVESTAD p.256) (DGA obituary) (KJR) (Wisconsin Cemetery Records)

ANDERSON, Peter WI 31st Inf. Co. B. Residence: Wiota, Lafayette County, Wisconsin. Born in Lafayette County, Wisconsin. Civil War: Age 21. Farmer. Dark eyes, fair hair, fair complexion, 5'8". Enlisted for three years on 8 Sep. 1863 at Madison, Wisconsin. Mustered 12 Sep. 1863 at Madison. Private. Awarded Medal of Honor for gallant conduct in saving, entirely unassisted, an artillery piece of the 14th Corps from capture at Bentonville, North Carolina, on 19 Mar. 1865. Transferred to Company K on 20 Jun. 1865. Promoted to corporal that day. Mustered out 8 July 1865 near Louisville, Kentucky. Sources: (SHSW Series 1200, boxes 145-4; 259-1; *Red Book*, vol. 36) (*America's Medal of Honor Recipients*, 1977, p. 20)

BERGH, John J. WI 25th Inf. Co. K. Residence: Bloomingdal, Vernon County, Wisconsin. Born in Norway. Civil War: Age 19. Farmer. Unmarried. Blue eyes, brown hair, fair complexion, 5'9." Enlisted for three years on 14 Aug. 1862 at Viroqua, Wisconsin, and mustered at La Crosse, Wisconsin, on 14 Sep. 1862. Private. Sources: (SHSW *Red Book*, vol. 30)

BJORN, Ludvig Marinus WI 15th Inf. Co. F. Born 7 Sep. 1835 in Moss, Norway. His father was a clergyman. Bjorn became a clergyman in 1861, moved to America and was installed as a pastor in Manitowoc County, Wisconsin. Civil War: He and many of his congregation formed Company F. After the war, he moved to Goodhue County, Minnesota, to serve congregations at Land and Minneola. Sources: (O. N. Nelson, *History of the Scandinavians in the United States*, Minneapolis, 1893. p.338)

BROWN, Robert US Navy. Born 1830 in Norway. Civil War: Enlisted from New York. Captain of the Top. Awarded the Medal of Honor for action on board *U.S.S. Richmond* in Mobile Bay on 5 Aug. 1864. Cool and courageous at his station throughout the prolonged action. Brown rendered gallant service as his vessel trained her guns on Fort Morgan and on ships of the Confederacy despite extremely heavy return fire. He took part in the actions at Forts Jackson and St. Philip, with the Chalmette batteries, at the surrender of New Orleans and in the attacks on batteries below Vicksburg. Sources: (*America's Medal of Honor Recipients*, 1977, pp. 42, 1012)

CHRISTENSON, Hans WI 15th Inf. Co. F. Residence: Brown County, Wisconsin. Born in Denmark. Civil War: Age 27. Farmer. Married. Blue eyes, blond hair, fair complexion, 5'6." Enlisted for three years on 18 Nov. 1861 at Manitowoc, Wisconsin, and mustered at Madison, Wisconsin, on 12 Dec. 1861. Private. Left sick at Mississippi River Island No. 10, on 11 June 1862 and sent to hospital 20 July 1862. Was sick in Iuka, Mississippi, and Corinth, Mississippi, the same year; also Bowling Green, Kentucky, and Farmington, Mississippi, and in Cleveland, Ohio, on 1 Jan. 1863. Killed, shot through the heart, on Rocky Face Ridge in the battle of New Hope Church, Georgia, on 27 May 1864. Sources: (SHSW Series 1200, box 76-8,15; *Red Book*, vol. 20, p.86) (LOVE p.1081) (BUSLETT p.501) (ULVESTAD p.274) (AGER p.306) (MEEKER)

CHRISTOFERSON, Ole WI 3rd Inf. Co. B. Born in Norway. Civil War: Age 44. Farmer. Blue eyes, brown hair, ruddy complexion, 5'5." Drafted. Enrolled at Carlton, Kewaunee County, Wisconsin, on 31 Oct. 1864 and mustered there the same day. Private. "Paid for arrest and delivery $14.50. Never reported to company for duty." Sources: (SHSW *Red Book*, vol. 9, p.42)

EMMONSON, Albert WI 15th Inf. Co. C. Residence: Norway Township, Racine County, Wisconsin. Born there. Civil War: Age 18. Unmarried. Enlisted for three years on 11 Oct. 1861 at Milwaukee, Wisconsin. Mustered 2 Dec. 1861 at Madison, Wisconsin. Corporal. Served as an escort with the provision transport from Stevenson, Alabama, on 13 Oct. 1863. Served as hospital steward. Promoted to sergeant on 7 Nov. 1864. Mustered out with company, 1 Jan. 1865, at Chattanooga, Tennessee. Was named Brevet (Honorary) Captain 20 Aug. 1867, effective from 20 Sep. 1863, because of bravery in battle at Chickamauga, when, after his captain was killed, he took a position in front of his company and encouraged his men by both word and deed to hold their ground even though they were hard pressed on all sides. Brother of Thomas Emmonson. Sources: (SHSW Series 1200, box 76-5; *Red Book*, vol. 20, p. 42) (BUSLETT p.411) (ULVESTAD p.253) (AGER p.73, photo; p.298) (MEEKER) (Richard J. Fapso, *Norwegians in Wisconsin*, Madison: Wisconsin Historical Society Press, 2001, p.21, photo) "Emerson, Albert" "Emonson, Albert" "Emmerson, Albert"

EMMONSON, Thomas WI 15th Inf. Co. C. Residence: Norway Township, Racine County, Wisconsin. Civil War: Age 21. Unmarried. Enlisted for three years on 31 Oct. 1861 at Waterford, Wisconsin. Mustered 2 Dec. 1861 at Madison, Wisconsin. Private. Wagoner with the provision transport on 20 June 1863. Was in Division Quartermaster Corps from 30 June 1863. Died of disease at Stevenson, Alabama, 19 Oct. 1863. Brother of Albert Emmonson. Sources: (SHSW Series 1200, box 76-5; *Red Book*, vol. 20, p. 44) (BUSLETT p.411) (ULVESTAD p.278) (AGER p.139, photo; p.298) "Emerson, Thomas"

FLEISCHER, Fredrik WI 15th Inf. Co. A. Residence: Chicago, Illinois. Born in Voss, Norway. Civil War: Unmarried. Enlisted for three years on 26 Oct. 1861 at Chicago. Mustered 15 Nov. 1861 at Madison, Wisconsin. Corporal. Discharged from the service at Stevenson, Alabama, 26 Aug. 1863, by order of Major General Halleck, so he could return to Norway to claim an inheritance. He hired a substitute, Hubbard Hammock, to take his place. Entered in Roll of Honor on 14 Feb. 1865. Postwar: Went back to his childhood home in Gudvangen, Voss, Norway, and ran a hotel. Died in 1906. Sources: (SHSW Series 1200, box 76-3; *Red Book*, vol. 20, p.16, *Blue Book*, vol. 20, p.14) (BUSLETT p.350) (ULVESTAD p.263) (AGER p.291) (GJERTVEIT) (MEEKER)

GILBERT, Neils J. WI 15th Inf. Co. F. Residence: Manitowoc, Manitowoc County, Wisconsin. Born "Nils Iversen Vaarum" at Vaarom farm, Østre Slidre, Valdres, Norway, 1842. Came to U.S. in 1857. Civil War: Age 20. Unmarried. Enlisted for three years on 2 Oct. 1861 at Manitowoc. Mustered 12 Dec. 1861 at Madison, Wisconsin, as sergeant. Transferred to WI 15th Inf. Co. A on 13 Jan. 1862. Promoted first sergeant 11 Nov. 1862. Wounded in his hip in the battle of Stones River, Tennessee, 31 Dec. 1862. Prisoner of war (?). In hospital at Nashville, Tennessee. Commissioned first lieutenant in WI 15th Inf. Co. A on 19 Oct. 1864. Discharged from the service 20 Dec. 1864. Entered on Roll of Honor for leading three men through rebel lines to recover a wounded soldier who had been left on the battlefield. (Letter describing his wounding is in Buslett, p.341.) Postwar: He lived in South Dakota and Montana, as postmaster and merchant. In 1893, he returned to Wisconsin, to Blair. Later he lived at Eleva, Wisconsin. Sources: (SHSW Series 1200, box 76-3,8; *Red Book*, vol. 20, p.14, p.84) (BUSLETT p. 341) (ULVESTAD p.257) (AGER p.74, photo; p.80, photo; p.232, photo; p.290; p.306) (MEEKER) (HEDBERG) "Gilbert, Nels I"

GRINAGER, Mons WI 15th Inf. Co. K. Residence: Bath Township, Freeborn County, Minnesota. Born on Grinager Farm, Tingelstad Parish, Hadeland, Norway, on 7 Oct. 1832, to Hans Pedersen Grinager and his wife Marthe. He came to America from Brandbu, Hadeland, in 1853 and worked on a farm owned by an American. He later went to Decorah, Winneshiek County, Iowa, where he worked in a mercantile business for about three years. In 1859, he moved to Freeborn County, Minnesota, and became a farmer. He married Anna Egge, daughter of Anders Egge. Civil War: Age 29. Grinager volunteered and was commissioned a captain at Madison, Wisconsin, on 30 Jan. 1862. He organized Company K, enrolling men from Manchester, Hartland, Bath and Freeborn Townships of Freeborn County. He was mustered at Madison on 11 Feb. 1862. In the battle of Stones River, Tennessee, his company had been scattered by enemy fire. He was wounded in a leg but stayed to put his company in order before seeking medical aid. He was sent to a hospital in nearby Murfreesboro, which was overrun by enemy soldiers the next day. Grinager remained their prisoner for five days until the

Confederate troops were forced to flee. He avoided being taken away with the other prisoners by crawling into an out-of-the-way hiding place. On sick leave for 20 days, 23 Jan. 1863. Worked as a recruiter in November 1863. Mustered out with K Company, 10 Feb. 1865, at Chattanooga, Tennessee. He returned to farming in Freeborn County, where he became well-to-do, owning several farms. He also became a banker. A veteran by this name, living in Worthington, Nobles County, Minnesota, was granted a pension of $15 a month because of a wound to his left leg. He died in 1889 in Minneapolis. His wife, Anne Egge, died about 1910. One son, Alexander Grinager, became known for his oil paintings. Sources: (SHSW Series 1200, box 76-12; *Red Book*, vol. 20, p.140) (BUSLETT p.614 photo) (ULVESTAD p.253) (AGER p.190 photo; p.316) (O. N. Nelson, *History of the Scandinavians in the United States*, Minneapolis, 1893. p.410) (FCHS) (LONN) (*Pensioners on the Roll as of January 1, 1883, Living in Minnesota*, Brooklyn Park, MN: Park Genealogical Books, 1994) "Greenager, Mons"

GUNDERSON, Edward LA 6th Inf. Co. I. Confederate. Residence: New Orleans, Louisiana. Born 20 Dec. 1837 in Solor, Norway. Immigrated in 1859 to Wisconsin. Worked in lumber camps until the spring of 1860. Started for Pike's Peak to search for gold. At Hannibal, Missouri, he met miners returning from Colorado who were broke and starving. Gunderson went to St. Louis and worked at odd jobs for a few weeks and then took passage on a boat to New Orleans. Worked as a laborer. Civil War: Drafted. Enrolled at New Orleans on 21 Mar. 1862. He was then 25 and unmarried, with blue eyes, auburn hair and a florid complexion, 5'9." Private. Sent to join the LA 6th Infantry in Virginia. He was captured by Union troops at Fredericksburg, Virginia, 5 May 1863 and sent to Fort Delaware. Exchanged 3 June 1863. He was wounded at Gettysburg on 2 July 1863. Escaped capture and was with his company through April 1864. Captured at the Battle of the Wilderness on 5 May 1864 and sent to Point Lookout prison, then transferred to Elmira, New York, until the war ended and he was released on 19 June 1865. He married in 1873 to Olivia Kalgaarden. Seven children. He moved to Kensett, Worth County, Iowa, and died there on 27 Jan. 1924. He is buried at Elk Creek Cemetery west of Kensett. Sources: (James P. Gannon, *Irish Rebels, Confederate Tigers*, 1998) (Obituary, "The Northwood Anchor") (WALK)

HALVORSEN, Kittel WI Heavy Artillery, First Regiment, Co. C. Residence: Winchester, Winnebago County, Wisconsin. Born "Kittel Halvorsen Kjeldahl" on 15 Dec. 1846 at Tuddal, Hjartdal, Telemark, Norway. Came to America with his parents at age two. Settled first near Whitewater, Walworth County, Wisconsin. Civil War: Age 17. Unmarried. Farmer. Blue eyes, light hair, light complexion, 5'6". Enlisted for three years on 5 Sep. 1863 at Winchester. Mustered 1 Oct. 1863 at Milwaukee, Wisconsin. Private. Fought in the Battle of Mission Ridge. Wounded. Promoted to corporal 24 Mar. 1865. After the war, he homesteaded near Belgrade in Stearns County, Minnesota. Elected to the Minnesota Legislature in 1885. Elected as a Populist to U.S. Congress in 1890. Defeated in 1892. In 1907, he was living in Marlow, South Dakota. Died in Havana, North Dakota, on 12 July 1936 and is buried at Big Grove Church Cemetery near Brooten, Minnesota. Sources: (SHSW *Red Book*, vol. 6) (ULVESTAD p.263) (O. N. Nelson, *History of the Scandinavians in the United States*, Minneapolis, 1893, p.419) (Biographical Directory of the United States Congress) "Halvorson, Kittel"

HAMMOCK, Hubbard WI 15th Inf. Co. A. Residence: Not shown. Civil War: Age 20. Private. Substitute for Corporal Fredrik Fleischer. (see FLEISCHER, Fredrik). Enrolled for three years and mustered 26 Aug. 1863 at Stevenson, Alabama, to serve the remainder of Fleischer's term, which began 26 Oct. 1861. Private. Wounded in Battle of Chickamauga, Georgia, 20 Sep. 1863, and sent to the general hospital in Chattanooga, Tennessee. Moved to a hospital in Louisville, Kentucky, and was still there on 24 Aug. 1864. Discharged from the service 20 Dec. 1864, at Chattanooga, Tennessee. Sources: (SHSW Series 1200, box 76-3; *Red Book*, vol. 20, p.16; *Blue Book*, vol. 20, p.14) (BUSLETT p.353) "Hammock, Edward"

HANSON, Knud WI First Cavalry Co. F. Residence: Winchester, Wisconsin. Born in Norway. Civil War: Age 33. Laborer. Blue eyes, light hair, ruddy complexion, 5'8". Drafted 24 Nov. 1863 and mustered the same day at Green Bay, Wisconsin. Private. Captured 30 July 1864. Died in Andersonville prison 28 Apr. 1865, the "last known" prisoner to die there. After his burial, two "unknowns" were buried. Sources: (William Marvel, *Andersonville, the Last Depot*, University of North Carolina Press, 1994, p.5)

HANSON, Ole IA 13th Inf. Co. C. Residence: Winneshiek County, Iowa. Born 15 Sep. 1840 on Pladsen, Lower Ness, Norway, to Hans Anderson Elefsrud and Kari Jensdatter. Arrived U.S. in August 1862. Civil War: Age 24. Enlisted 31 Oct. 1864. Mustered 31 Oct. 1864. Private. Mustered out 21 July 1865, Louisville, Kentucky. Later, took name "O. H. Nass." Died 26 Dec. 1919. Buried in Glenwood Cemetery, Glenwood Township, Winneshiek County. Sources: (ISW-II p.622) (O. H. Nass diary, in Vesterheim library) (DGA) (Wisconsin Cemetery Records) (HEDBERG) "Nass, Ole H."

HANSON, Ole Knudsen WI 15th Inf. Co. A. Residence: Boone County, Illinois. Born 2 Jan. 1837 at Seljord, Telemark, Norway. Came with his parents to America in 1842. Civil War: Unmarried. Enlisted for three years on 15 Oct. 1861 at Chicago, Illinois. Mustered 15 Nov. 1861 at Madison, Wisconsin. Sergeant. Sick in hospital in Mound City, Illinois. Reported on 3 June 1862 to be on home leave. Assigned to the division supply train 16 Aug. 1863. Sick in hospital in Knoxville, Tennessee since 22 Feb. 1864. Wounded in the battle of New Hope Church, Georgia, 27 May 1864 and was left on the battlefield. He was taken up by rebel troops and held prisoner. Was still absent as a prisoner of war at time of muster out of his regiment. Was crippled the rest of his life. Was made a Brevet (Honorary) Captain on 22 May 1867 with rank retroactive to 27 May 1864 "in recognition of distinguished gallantry displayed by him at the battle of Dallas (New Hope Church) where although wounded five times he refused to leave the fields and finally fell into the hands of the enemy, he having advanced so far forward that it was impossible for his regiment to reach and save him." Postwar: Married 22 May 1866 in Boone County, Illinois. Died 18 Dec. 1882 at Furnas County, Nebraska. Sources: (SHSW Series 1200, box 76-3; *Red Book*, vol. 20, p.16; *Blue Book*, vol. 20, p.14) (BUSLETT p.352) (AGER p.292) (GRIMSRUD) (ULVESTAD p.254, 288) (QUINER p. 629) (MEEKER) (www.ancestry.com) (HEDBERG) "Hams, O. K."

HEG, Hans Christian WI 15th Inf. Residence: Waterford, Racine County, Wisconsin. Born in Lier, near Drammen, Norway, on 21 Dec. 1829, son of Even Hansen Heg, an innkeeper, and Siri Olsdatter Heg. To U.S. 1840. Settled at Muskego, Wisconsin. Hans was married, 1851, to Gunhild Einung, who was born in Tinn, Telemark, Norway, in 1834, and who came to America at age 8 in 1842. She lived until 1923. Civil War: Age 32. Hans Heg was commissioned a colonel on 30 Sep. 1861. Mustered 13 Feb. 1862 at Madison, Wisconsin. Organized and commanded the 15th Wisconsin Regiment. Left sick on 30 Oct. 1862 at Cave City, Kentucky. Promoted 28 Feb. 1863 to command the Second Brigade, Davis' Division, 1st Division, 20th Corps, Army of the Cumberland. Mortally wounded in Battle at Chickamauga, Georgia, 19 Sep. 1863, and died the next morning. Heg is buried in the Muskego Cemetery, Racine County, Wisconsin. Sources: (SHSW Series 1200,boxes 76-2, 78-1; *Red Book*, vol. 20, p. 10) (BUSLETT p.295, photo) (ONI p.60) (ULVESTAD p.251) (AGER p.289) (MEEKER) (HEDBERG)

HELGESON, Carl WI 1st Cavalry, Co. D. Born in Norway in August 1845. Came to America in 1860. Civil War: Enrolled 14 Sep. 1864 at Eau Claire, Wisconsin. Mustered 8 Oct. 1864 at Madison, Wisconsin. Private. Discharged from the service 19 July 1865 at Edgefield, Tennessee. On 9 Dec. 1870, he married Sigvi "Sarah" Severtsen in Colfax, Wisconsin. In 1871, the couple homesteaded north of Montevideo, Minnesota. They had four children. In 1879, Carl left his family, moved to Campbell, Nebraska, changed his name to Charley Johnson (Jansen), and married a woman who used the names "Mary" and "Jennie," who had gone there with him from Minnesota. They had five children. Helgeson died 27 Aug. 1910, and was buried in the military cemetery at the Presidio, San Francisco, California, grave 1458, west side new addition. Sources: (Family history of Carl Helgeson Alapmoen by Arthur V. and Audrey C. Helgeson, Loveland, Colorado, pub. 9 Dec. 1995) "Helgeson, Karel" "Johnson, Charley"

HOLBERG, Edward WI 15th Inf. Co. A. Residence: Chicago, Illinois. Civil War: Age 35. Married. Enlisted for three years on 18 Oct. 1861 at Chicago. Mustered 15 Nov. 1861 at Madison, Wisconsin. Private. Absent under arrest 17 May 1862, following a *Syttende Mai* party at Mississippi River Island No. 10. Left sick at Iuka, Mississippi, on 21 Aug. 1862. Left sick in hospital at Lebanon, Kentucky, 27 Oct. 1862. Sick and sent to hospital in Murfreesboro 2 Apr. 1863. Assigned to escort a supply train from Stevenson, Alabama, beginning 13 Oct. 1863. Absent sick in Nashville since 26 Oct. 1863. Absent sick in Chattanooga, Tennessee, since 11 May 1864. Absent, assigned to an ordnance detail in Chattanooga, 15 Sep. 1864. Mustered out with A Company at Chattanooga on 20 Dec. 1864. Sources: (SHSW Series 1200, box 76-3; *Red Book*, vol. 20, p.16; *Blue Book*, vol. 20, p.14) (BUSLETT p.354) (ULVESTAD p.292) (AGER p.292) "Holberg, Edvard"

JENSON, Jens S. TX Cavalry. McCord's Frontier Regiment. Co. E. Confederate. Residence: Clifton, Bosque County, Texas. Born 28 Mar. 1835 in Brovold Prestegjeld, Arendal, Norway. Emigrated with his parents and six siblings to Bosque County, Texas, in 1853. Civil War: Drafted into the Confederate Army on 20 Dec. 1862 at Camp Salmon, Texas, and served four years. Private. There is a family story that after the war he buried his guns on his home farm and they have never been found. He died 3 Jan. 1912. Sources: (C.A. Clausen & Derwood Johnson, "Norwegian Soldiers in Confederate Forces," *Norwegian-American Studies*, vol. 25, Northfield: Norwegian-American Historical Association, p.114) (ULVESTAD p.295) (e-mail from grandson Maurice Jenson, Stillwater, Minnesota) "Jensen, G. S."

JOHNSON, George WI 15th Inf. Co. G. Residence: Beloit, Rock County, Wisconsin. Born "Guttorm Johnson Hovden" in Krodsherad, Norway, 29 Apr. 1831 (or 1835). Sometime following the deaths of his parents, he and an older brother came to America in 1852 and they settled at Long Prairie, Illinois. Civil War: Age 25. Unmarried. Enlisted for three years on 28 Sep. 1861 at Beloit and mustered at Madison, Wisconsin, 13 Dec. 1861. Assigned as sergeant. Promoted to first sergeant on 17 June 1863. On 28 Aug. 1863, he was given a 30-day furlough from Mississippi River Island No. 10, and he traveled to Beloit, where he was reported sick on 1 Sep. 1863. Mustered out 13 Jan. 1865. Commissioned second lieutenant 25 Feb. 1867, retroactive to 1 Oct. 1862. He said that he was named sergeant on his arrival in Camp Randall. He also said he received his officer's appointment in 1863, but was not given a commission at that time. He said he commanded Company G for 18 months, but was never paid for this. After the war, he took back his baptismal name, Guttorm, and his Norway farm name, Hovden, and he became a well-to-do farmer near Ridgeway, Winneshiek County, Iowa. Died 30 Jan. 1902. Buried in Madison Churchyard near Ridgeway. Sources: (SHSW Series 1200, box 76-9; *Red Book*, vol. 20, p.98) (BUSLETT p.525 photo) (DGA) (ULVESTAD p.296) (AGER p.271 photo) (GJERTVEIT) (JR) (Wisconsin Cemetery Records) "Hovden, Guttorm"

JOHNSON, Henry U.S. Navy. Born 1824 in Norway. Civil War: Enlisted from New York. Seaman. Awarded the Medal of Honor. As seaman on board the *U.S.S. Metacomet*, Johnson served as a member of the boat's crew which went to the rescue of the *U.S. Monitor Tecumseh* when that vessel was struck by a torpedo while passing the enemy forts in Mobile Bay on 5 Aug. 1864. He braved the enemy fire which was said by the admiral to be "one of the most galling" he had ever seen. Johnson aided in rescuing from death ten of the crew of the *Tecumseh*, eliciting admiration of friend and foe. Sources: (*America's Medal of Honor Recipients*, 1977, pp. 131, 1015)

JOHNSON, John WI 2nd Inf. Co. A. Residence: Janesville, Rock County, Wisconsin. Born 25 Mar. 1842 in Toten, Norway. Civil War: Age 18. Laborer. Unmarried. Blue eyes, light brown hair, fair complexion, 5'4". Enlisted for three years on 20 Apr. 1861 at Janesville. Mustered 11 June 1861 at Madison, Wisconsin. Private. Later entries show him in Company D. Private Johnson was in these battles: Bull Run 21 July 1861; Rappahanock Station 21, 22, 23 Aug. 1862; White Sulpher Springs, Virginia, 26 Aug. 1862; Gainesville, Virginia, 28 Aug. 1862; Bull Run, Virginia, 29, 30 Aug. 1862; South Mountain, Virginia, 14 Sep. 1862; Antietam, 17 Sep. 1862; and Fredericksburg, Virginia 13 Dec. 1862. He lost his right arm at Fredericksburg. Discharged from the service for disability, 10 Apr. 1863, at Belle Plain, Virginia. Postwar: Lived in Rochester, Minnesota. On 28 Aug. 1893, he was issued the Medal of Honor for conspicuous gallantry in battle of Antietam at Fredericksburg, the battle in which he was wounded. "While serving as cannoneer, he manned the positions of fallen gunners." Sources: (SHSW Series 1200, box 6; *Red Book*, vol. 8) (*America's Medal of Honor Recipients*, 1977, pp. 131, 1015) (*Medal of Honor Recipients 1863-1994*, vol. 1, no. 690, Facts on File, Inc., 1995) (QUINER p. 456)

JOHNSON, Osmund WI 15th Inf. Co. K. Residence: Fillmore County, Minnesota. Born 23 Feb. 1827 at Tvedt, Årdal, Rogaland, a son of Jan Eivindsson and Valborg Osmundsdatter. Married on 21 Apr. 1854 at Finnöy Parish to Barbro Kjeldsdatter Nådeöen. They came to America soon after marrying and settled in Rock County, Illinois. In 1858, they moved to a farm in Holt Township, Fillmore County, Minnesota. Civil War: Age 34. Married. He enlisted for three years on 11 Feb. 1862 in Fillmore County and mustered at Madison, Wisconsin, the same day(?). Private. Left behind sick at Mississippi River Island No. 10 on 11 June 1862. Sick in Bardstown, Kentucky, 7 Oct. 1862. Taken prisoner at Stones River, Tennessee, 31 Dec. 1862. Held in Libby Prison at Richmond, Virginia. In March, 1863, he was exchanged and sent to a parole camp at St. Louis, Missouri. He later rejoined his company. He was reported missing in action on 20 Sep. 1863 in the Battle of Chickamauga. He had been wounded in the back of his head and lay unconscious on the battlefield. He was picked up by the Confederate forces and taken to Richmond, and sent from there to Danville, Virginia, on 12 Dec. 1863. In Feb. 1864, he was moved to Andersonville Prison. Starvation and scurvy put him in the prison hospital 6 Aug. through 8 Sep. 1864. Sent to Millen, Georgia, on 11 Nov. 1864. He was released to Union authorities at Jacksonville, Florida, on 29 Apr. 1865. On his discharge from the service at Madison, Wisconsin, 30 May 1865, he went back to his home in Minnesota, where everyone believed he had died in prison. He arrived home just in time to stop the wedding of his wife to a neighbor. It is said that Barbro did not recognize him, he was so emaciated. He weighed about 60 pounds and could not stand. Postwar: On 15 Feb. 1888, Osmund was awarded a pension of $12 a month. Osmund and Barbro farmed in Holt Township until 1900, then moved to the town of Whalen, Fillmore County. His pension eventually reached $24 a month. He died 1 Oct. 1906, age 79, at the home of his son, John O. Johnson of Peterson, Fillmore County, Minnesota. His wife, Barbro, died 29 Jun. 1908. Osmund Johnson was a brother of Knud Johnson of the Minnesota 1st Regiment of Artillery, Company B. Sources: (SHSW Series 1200, box 76-12; *Red Book*, vol. 20, p.144) (BUSLETT p.631) (AGER p.171, photo; p.317) (GJERTVEIT) (ULVESTAD p.299) (MEEKER).

JOHNSON, Thomas MN 3rd Inf. Co. D. Residence: Dunkirk, Dane County, Wisconsin. Born "Thomas Johnsen Lehnskjoldgrav" on 27 Feb. 1824 at Lensegrav in Drangedal, Norway, to farmer Jon Halvorsen and Johanne Knudsdatter. He married Siri Einertsdatter Vraalstad on 26 Mar. 1846, in Drangedal Parish, Norway. Siri was born 27 July 1823 in Tordal Parish, Drangedal, to farmer Einert of Wraalstad and Kari Pedersdatter. Thomas and Siri came to America in 1846 and settled at Koshkonong Prairie, Wisconsin. They had six children: Johanna Karine, born 4 Jan. 1850; Elaine, born 14 July 1854 and who died 12 June 1908; Sivert (or Einert), born Feb. 1858; Halvor, born Sep. 1860; Andrea, born 26 Mar. 1864; and John, born Feb. 1866. Civil War: Age 37. Blue eyes, dark hair, dark complexion, 5'10". Enrolled for three years on 3 Oct. 1861 at Fort Snelling, Minnesota. Mustered 4 Nov. 1861 at Fort Snelling. Private. On 29 Mar. 1862, at Nashville, Tennessee, he was discharged from the service for disability due to "chronic rheumatism for which he has been frequently disabled for a few days at a time." His wife, Siri, was appointed her husband's guardian on 14 Oct. 1897, he being judged a spendthrift. They lived at Fisher, Minnesota, at the time. Johnson died 14 May 1905 at Garfield, Polk County, Minnesota, of Bright's Disease. In January, 1906, when she was 82, Siri Johnson applied for and was granted a widow's pension of $12 a month. She died 12 June 1908. Sources: (MINN p.137) (MCIW p.185) (Certificate of Disability for Discharge) (Information from pension papers, and from a descendant, Dr. Arthur G. Lensgraf, Nashville, Tennessee. Marriage and immigration dates may be in error, for Dr. Lensgraf has a letter written by Thomas Johnson Lensegrav, Dunkirk, Dane County, Wisconsin Territory, dated 20 Apr. 1846, saying they had arrived in Milwaukee 24 Aug. "last year.") [Death may have been at Fisher, Minnesota, or at Fertile, Minnesota.]

JONES, Kiler K. WI 15th Inf. Residence: Quincy, Illinois. Born in United States. Civil War: Age 37. Enrolled for three years on 26 Sep. 1861 at Quincy, Illinois. Commissioned lieutenant colonel, Wisconsin 15th, on 21 Dec. 1861. He was not Norwegian; his wife was. He recruited Company A in Chicago. Commission revoked 1 Mar. 1862. Mustered out of service on 2 Mar. 1862 per order of the War Department, but General Halleck would not recognize the muster out until 5 Mar. 1862. Lived at Manitowoc, Manitowoc County, Wisconsin. Sources: (SHSW Series 1200,boxes 76-2, 78-1; *Red Book*, vol. 20, p. 2) (BUSLETT p.317; LONN p.136) (GJERTVEIT) (TAR) (HEDBERG)

JULSON, Ole WI 50th Inf. Co. H. Residence: Waterloo, Grant County, Wisconsin. Born in Norway. Civil War: Farmer. Age 40. Married. Blue eyes, light hair, dark complexion, 5'9". Enlisted for one year on 10 Mar. 1865 at Boscobel, Wisconsin. Mustered there the same day. Bounty $100, $33.33 paid.

Private. "Captain Charles Cox, Company H, died 11 July 1865 from wounds received at hands of Private Ole Julson on board the steamer *Post Boy* on the Missouri River." "O. Julson jumped overboard from Steamer 'Post Boy' on Missouri River and supposed to be drowned." Unit was on its way from Jefferson, Missouri, to Fort Leavenworth, Kansas, at the time. Shooting took place near Boonville, Missouri. Sources: (SHSW Series 1200, box 195-9,17, Regimental Report of 31 July 1865)

KILLOE, Gunder MN 10th Inf. Co. D. Residence: Wanamingo, Goodhue County, Minnesota. Born in Norway. Civil War: Age 21. Enrolled 22 Aug. 1862. Mustered 9 Oct. 1862. Private. Disappeared on 8 Oct. 1863 from Fort Snelling, Minnesota. Listed as deserted. Sources: (MINN p.471) (MCIW p.478) "Killor, Gunder"

KNUDSEN, Knud From Stjernes, Rollag, Nummedal, Norway. Civil War: Private. Wounded in the Battle of Stones River, Tennessee [31 Dec. 1862-2 Jan. 1863]. Died at St. Olaf, Clayton County, Iowa, in 1874. Sources: (ULVESTAD p.302, 330)

KNUDSEN, Niels WI 15th Inf. Co. A. Residence: Chicago, Illinois. From Stavanger, Norway. Civil War: Age 27. Unmarried. Enlisted for three years on 28 Oct. 1861 at Chicago. Mustered 15 Nov. 1861 at Madison, Wisconsin. Private. Under arrest at Mississippi River Island No. 10 on 17 May 1862, disappeared from jail on 11 July 1862, and was never mustered out. Was said to be living in Norse, Texas, after the war. Sources: (SHSW Series 1200, box 76-3; *Red Book*, vol. 20, p.18) (BUSLETT p.358) (HEDBERG)

LARSON, Lars A. WI 15th Inf. Co. K. Residence: State Line, Freeborn County, Minnesota. Born in Norway. Came to America in 1852. Lived a year in Rock County, Wisconsin; then came to Freeborn County. Civil War: Age 29. Unmarried. Enlisted for three years on 12 Dec. 1861 in Freeborn County and mustered at Madison, Wisconsin, 11 Feb. 1862. Designated corporal on 1 Feb. 1862. Promoted to sergeant 1 July 1862. Sick in hospital at Iuka, Mississippi, in October 1862. Wounded and taken prisoner at Chickamauga, Georgia, 19 Sep. 1863. Sick at Benton Barracks in St. Louis, Missouri, in October 1864. Mustered out at Madison, Wisconsin, 20 Feb. 1865. Was named Brevet (Honorary) Second Lieutenant 25 Feb. 1867, with rank retroactive to 10 Nov. 1864, for courage in helping mortally wounded Colonel Heg from the Chickamauga battlefield. Returned to Freeborn County after the war. Sources: (SHSW Series 1200, box 76-12; *Red Book*, vol. 20, p.140) (BUSLETT p.632) (ULVESTAD p.258) (MEEKER) (HEDBERG)

LARSON, Stark WI 15th Inf. Co. B. Residence: Pleasant Spring, Dane County, Wisconsin. Born in Voss, Norway. Civil War: Age 36. Married. Enlisted for three years on 23 Oct. 1861 at Madison, Wisconsin, and mustered there on 20 Nov. 1861. Private. Left behind because of illness at Mississippi River Island No. 10, in June, 1862. Sick in hospital at Iuka, Mississippi, August 1862. Discharged from the service for disability, Quincy, Illinois, 11 May 1863. Died in Kandiyohi County, Minnesota (before 1907). Sources: (SHSW Series 1200, box 76-4; *Red Book*, vol. 20, p. 32) (BUSLETT p.388) (RWV p.809) (AGER p.296) (ULVESTAD p.305)

LUND, Christian Born in Farsund, Norway, in 1839. Grew up in Oslo. Went to sea in 1858 on the bark *Deodota* and did not return to Norway until 1911 when he made a visit. Civil War: Came on a ship to New Orleans during the Civil War and was pressed into Confederate service. He escaped and entered the Union Navy. He is said to have been the only Norwegian sailor on record to see service under Flag Officer Foote and General Grant on the Tennessee and Cumberland Rivers, when the Confederates surrendered Forts Henry and Donelson to the Union Army. Later he served under Admiral Porter at Vicksburg. Subsequently he enlisted as a soldier and fought at Petersburg, where he lost a finger. He became a lieutenant and, after the war, was raised to captain. He became a sailing master on the Great Lakes, living in Oswego, New York. He eventually retired to New York City. Sources: (RYGG p.52)

NELSON, Ben WI 15th Inf. Co. I. Residence: Elk Mound, Eau Claire County, Wisconsin. Born Bersven Nilson at Ovre Fleskemo, Maalselvedalen, Troms, Finnmark, Norway. Came to America in 1861 to La Crosse, Wisconsin, with his parents and ten siblings. Civil War: Age 19. Unmarried. Enlisted 8 Nov. 1861 at Withon, Wisconsin, and mustered at Madison, Wisconsin, 20 Dec. 1861. Private. On sick leave in Eau Claire, Wisconsin, in May, 1862. Was with the provisions transport from Stevenson, Alabama, in Sept. and Oct. 1863. Was on military police duty on 23 May 1864. Mustered out with I Company at Chattanooga, Tennessee, 10 Feb. 1865. Lived at West Superior, Wisconsin. Sources: (SHSW Series 1200, box 76-11; *Red Book*, vol. 20, p.132) (BUSLETT p.600) (AGER p.315; p.15, photo) (ULVESTAD p.313) (GJERTVEIT) "Nelson, Bersven"

NELSON, Charles B. WI 15th Inf. Co. G. Residence: Beloit, Rock County, Wisconsin. Civil War: Age 35. Married. Enlisted 27 Sep. 1861 and mustered at Madison, Wisconsin, on 13 Dec. 1861 as first sergeant of the company. Detached with his company at Mississippi River Island No. 10. Was a witness in a general military court in Columbus, Kentucky, 17 May 1863. Commissioned first lieutenant 17 June 1863 in Chattanooga, Tennessee, with rank from 21 Jan. 1863 at Mississippi River Island No. 10. Was company commander for awhile in 1863. Was with the provision transport from Stevenson, Alabama, during Oct., 1863. Seriously wounded in his right shoulder at New Hope Church, Georgia, 27 May 1864, and was sent to hospital in Nashville, Tennessee. Mustered out with G Company at Chattanooga, Tennessee, on 13 Jan. 1865. Sources: (SHSW Series 1200, box 76-9; *Red Book*, vol. 20, p.98) (BUSLETT p.524) (ULVESTAD p.258) (AGER p.311)

NELSON, Hans A. IA 3rd Inf. Co. D. Residence: Decorah, Winneshiek County, Iowa. Born at Stubberud in Feiring near Mjosen, Norway. Civil War: Age 22. Enlisted 20 May 1861. Mustered 8 June 1861. Private. Wounded slightly in his left side on 12 July 1863 in the battle of Jackson, Mississippi. Mustered out 17 June 1864, Davenport, Iowa, expiration term of service. Postwar: A veteran of this name, living in West Brook, Cottonwood County, Minnesota, was granted a pension of $4 for a gunshot wound to his right side. Died at Revere, Minnesota, in 1905. Sources: (ISW-I p.363) (ULVESTAD p.312) (*Pensioners on the Roll as of January 1, 1883, Living in Minnesota*, Brooklyn Park, MN: Park Genealogical Books, 1994) [See also IA 13th Inf. Co. H]

NELSON, Harvey WI 29th Inf. Co. A. Residence: Waterloo, Jefferson County, Wisconsin. Civil War: Age 30. Enlisted for three years on 21 Aug. 1862 at Waterloo. Mustered 27 Sept. 1862 at Madison, Wisconsin. Private. Appointed wagoner. Reduced to ranks 29 Nov. 1864. Mustered out on 22 June 1865 at Shreveport, Louisiana. Sources: (SHSW *Red Book*, vol. 34)

NELSON, Knute WI 4th Inf. Co. B. Born Evanger, Voss, Norway, on 2 Feb. 1843. In 1849, he came with his mother to Chicago, where he sold newspapers to help support himself and his mother. Moved to Dane County, Wisconsin, fall of 1850. Entered Albion Academy in 1858. Civil War: Age 18. Enlisted 2 July 1861 (or May 1861) at Racine, Wisconsin. Mustered the same day. Private. Assigned to Company B. Wounded and taken prisoner in the siege at Port Hudson, Louisiana, 14 June 1863. He remained a prisoner until the place surrendered on 9 July 1863. Promoted to corporal. Discharged from the service 14 July 1864, his term having expired. He married in 1867 Nicholina Jacobsen at Christiana, Wisconsin. They moved to Alexandria, Minnesota. Homesteaded 120 acres of farm land. Admitted to the bar in 1867. Elected to the U.S. Congress in 1882. Served three terms. Elected Governor of Minnesota in 1892. Became U.S. Senator and served five terms, 1895 to 1923. Died 28 Apr. 1923 on board a train from Washington to Minnesota. Sources: (Memorial address to the Senate by Senator Henrik Shipstead of Minnesota.) (ULVESTAD p.264) (O. N. Nelson, *History of the Scandinavians in the United States*, Minneapolis, 1893, p.510) (ONI p.61) (LONN p.159) (DCHS 1890 Veterans Census card file)

NORDE, Martin J. WI 15th Inf. Co. I. Residence: Scandinavia, Waupaca County, Wisconsin. Born at Nyflodt, Ringebu, Norway, about 1842, the son of Johans Mortensen Nyflodt. Affectionately called "Lillemorten." Civil War: Age 19. Enlisted for three years on 20 Nov. 1861 at Scandinavia and mustered at Madison, Wisconsin, 20 Dec. 1861. Private. Was with the provisions transport from Stevenson, Alabama, in Oct. 1863. Was sent on recruiting duty on 21 Nov. 1863. Promoted to sergeant of ordnance (orderly?) on 1 Jan. 1865. Promoted to first sergeant on 1 Jan. 1865. Mustered out

10 Feb. 1865. Postwar: Norde became a successful businessman in Alexandria, Minnesota. He died there. Sources: (SHSW Series 1200, box 76-11; *Red Book*, vol. 20, p.126) (DCHS 1890 Veterans Census card file) (BUSLETT p.602 photo) (MEEKER) (AGER p.154, photo; p.315) (ULVESTAD p.260) (GJERTVEIT) "Nordre, Martin" "Nordre, Morten" "Jensson, Morten"

OLSON, Ebrah WI 30th Inf. Co. C. Residence: Preston, Trempealeau County, Wisconsin. Born in Norway. Civil War: Age 18. Farmer. Unmarried. Blue eyes, light hair, light complexion, 5'10". Enlisted for three years on 15 Aug. 1862 at Galesville, Wisconsin. Mustered 21 Oct. 1862 at Madison, Wisconsin. Private. He was killed during a draft riot in New Lisbon, Wisconsin, on 10 Sep. 1863, shot twice in his left breast by a revolver. Buried in Madison. Sources: (SHSW Series 1200, box 140-13; *Red Book*, vol. 35) (LARSEN p.49) (LOVE p.1108) (Kennedy, James B. Wisconsin Civil War name index) "Oleson, Ebrat" "Olson, Ebrat"

OLSON, Olaf WI 15th Inf. Co. A. Residence: Chicago, Illinois. Civil War: Age 19. Unmarried. Enlisted for three years on 8 Oct. 1861 at Chicago. Mustered 15 Nov. 1861 at Madison, Wisconsin. Private. He was in jail at Mississippi River Island No. 10 on 17 May 1862. Sick in Nashville. Transferred to the Navy near Ringgold, Georgia, 5 May 1864. Sources: (SHSW Series 1200, box 76-3; *Red Book*, vol. 20, p. 20) (BUSLETT p.364) (AGER p.293)

OLSON, Sven TX. Civil War: Confederate. Residence: Brownsboro, Texas. Born in Tovdal, Norway, 1821, the son of Ole Aslakson. Sven married Asborg. The couple, along with Sven's father, came to America in 1846 in a group led by Johan Reierson. At Alexandria, Louisiana, they could not afford a wagon to haul their possessions, so Sven made a wheelbarrow from a large log. He walked and pushed the wheelbarrow, while his wife, Asborg, walked beside him, carrying their infant child. The child died on the trip. The couple eventually reached Brownsboro. Three daughters were born there. Civil War: Enlisted at beginning of the war. Private. Served 18 months. Assigned to Vicksburg. He was at Shiloh. Sven died in 1906, age 84. Asborg died in 1894. Sources: (Alice Marie Nelson, *The Nelson-Jorgenson Saga*, privately printed, 1950.)

OYEN, Anthon Odin WI 15th Inf. Residence: Chicago, Illinois. Born in Trondhjem, Norway, 8 Oct. 1841. Was pharmacist in Bodø, Norway. Came to America in 1861. Civil War: Age 21. Enlisted for three years on 8 Oct. 1861. Private. Appointed hospital steward on 18 Nov. 1861 and mustered at Madison, Wisconsin, 13 Feb. 1862. Served as hospital pharmacist. Taken prisoner in Battle of Chickamauga, Georgia, on 20 Sept. 1863, and spent 18 months in Southern prisons, including Andersonville. Exchanged out of Andersonville on 1 Apr. 1865. Mustered out at Madison, Wisconsin, 25 May 1865. Returned to Chicago. Spent 20 years in the city police force. Lived until 1892; died at home of a heart attack. Sources: (SHSW Series 1200, boxes 76-2, 78-1; *Red Book*, vol. 20, p. 4) (BUSLETT p. 333; p.649 photo) (ULVESTAD p.253). (AGER p.237 photo) (ancestry.com) "Oien, Anthon" "Øyen, Anthon"

PETERSON, Henry WI 11th Inf. Co. K. Residence: Winchester, Winnebago County, Wisconsin. Born 28 Jan. 1849 in Tuddal, Telemark, Norway, a son of Sven Peterson and Anne Sørensdatter Hovland. Civil War: Age 18 (he was actually 15). Farmer. Unmarried. Blue eyes, light hair, fair complexion, 5'11." Enlisted for three years on 22 Feb. 1864 at Green Bay, Wisconsin. Mustered there the same day. Bounty $300. Volunteer recruit. Private. Took part with the WI 23rd Inf. in General Banks' Red River campaign in 1864. Took part in the siege and capture of Fort Blakely, Alabama, 9 Apr. 1865. Discharged 4 Sept. 1865. On 2 Jan. 1869 he married Anne Hansdatter Twito. They lived in Minnesota, just north of Highlandville, Winneshiek County, Iowa, for ten years, then in the Dakotas, Nebraska, Colorado and eventually in Lake Mills, Winnebago County, Iowa. Granted pension, which eventually reached $50 per month. Died 16 Nov. 1925 in Lake Mills. Buried at North Lutheran Cemetery, Lake Mills. Sources: (SHSW Series 1200, box 52-13; *Red Book*, vol. 16, p.204) (Discharge certificate, death certificate, pension drop certificate, and newspaper article all furnished by Hamlet A. Peterson, Jr., Rochester, Minnesota)

PETERSON, John IA 37th Inf. Co. C. Residence: Keokuk, Iowa. Born in Norway. Civil War: Age 45. Enlisted 9 Nov. 1862. Mustered 27 Oct. 1862. Private. The 37th was known as 'The Graybeards' and the 'Silver Grays.' The minimum age of enlistees was 45, the average age 57, the oldest was an 80-year-old man from Muscatine, Iowa, named Curtis King. The 37th was assigned guard duty at railroads around St. Louis, Missouri; then to guard the prison in Alton, Illinois, and later to guard supply trains near Memphis, Tennessee. Their final assignment was to guard prisoners in Ohio. The unit, including Peterson, was mustered out 24 May 1865, at Davenport, Iowa. Sources: (ISW-V p.805) (IVAL p.483)

PHINNEY, William US Navy. Born 1824 in Norway. Civil War: Enlisted from New York. Boatswain's Mate. Awarded Medal of Honor. On board the U.S.S. *Lackawanna* during successful attacks against Fort Morgan, rebel gunboats and the ram *Tennessee* in Mobile Bay on 5 Aug. 1864. Serving as a gun captain, Phinney showed much presence of mind in managing the gun and gave much needed encouragement to the crew during the engagement which resulted in the capture of the prize rebel ram *Tennessee* and the damaging and destruction of Fort Morgan. Sources: (*America's Medal of Honor Recipients*, 1977, pp.189, 1019)

ROBINSON, Thomas US Navy. Born 17 May 1837 in Norway. No War: Enlistment credited to New York. Captain of the Afterguard. Awarded the Medal of Honor for heroic efforts to save from drowning Wellington Brocar, landsman, of the *Tallapoosa*, off New Orleans on 15 July 1866. Sources: (*America's Medal of Honor Recipients*, 1977, pp.328, 1019)

SAMPSON, Samuel WI 15th Inf. Co. A. Residence: Boone County, Illinois. Civil War: Age 22. Unmarried. Enlisted for three years on 16 Oct. 1861 in Boone County and mustered at Madison, Wisconsin, 15 Nov. 1861. Private. Died of disease at Mississippi River Island No. 10 on 30 May 1862, and is buried in the Mississippi River Cemetery near Memphis, Tennessee. Sources: (SHSW Series 1200, box 76-3; *Red Book*, vol. 20, p.20) (BUSLETT p.263 English) (ULVESTAD p.326) (MEEKER)

SAMPSON, Thomas WI 15th Inf. Co. A. Residence: Boone County, Illinois. Civil War: Age 20. Unmarried. Enlisted for three years on 16 Oct. 1861 in Boone County. Mustered 15 Nov. 1861 at Madison, Wisconsin. Private. Died of disease at Mississippi River Island No. 10 on 23 May 1862. Buried in Mississippi River Cemetery near Memphis, Tennessee. Sources: (SHSW Series 1200, box 76-3; *Red Book*, vol. 20, p.20) (BUSLETT p.365) (ULVESTAD p.327) (AGER p.293)

SOMME, Gabriel E. WI 15th Inf. Co. A. Residence: Chicago, Illinois. Civil War: Age 22. Married. Enlisted for three years on 24 Dec. 1861 at Chicago. Mustered 1 Jan. 1862 at Madison, Wisconsin. Private. Seriously wounded at Stones River, Tennessee, 31 Dec. 1862, and sent to Nashville, Tennessee. In Convalescent Hospital in Murfreesboro, Tennessee, 17 May 1863. Sick in Knoxville, Tennessee, 14 Jan. 1864. Sick in Chattanooga, 2 May 1864. Sick in hospital at Jefferson, Indiana. Wounded in the Battle of New Hope Church and taken prisoner, 27 May 1864. Mustered out 20 Dec. 1864. Sources: (SHSW Series 1200, box 76-3; *Red Book*, vol. 20, p.20) (BUSLETT p.366) (ULVESTAD p.329) (AGER p.293) (ancestry.com)

SOMME, Gabriel J. WI 15th Inf. Co. A. Residence: Chicago, Illinois. Civil War: Age 43. Unmarried. Enlisted for three years on 25 Oct. 1861 at Chicago. Mustered 15 Nov. 1861 at Madison, Wisconsin. Private. Missing in Battle of Stones River, Tennessee, 31 Dec. 1862. Came back to the regiment. Promoted to corporal. Sick at Knoxville, Tennessee, 28 Nov. 1863. Sick at Knoxville 24 Feb. 1864. Taken prisoner in the Battle of New Hope Church, Georgia, 27 May 1864. Mustered out at Madison, Wisconsin, 6 Dec. 1864, at expiration of term of service. Sources: (SHSW *Red Book*, vol. 20, p.20) (BUSLETT p.266) (ULVESTAD p.329) (AGER p.293) (MEEKER)

STEEN, Charles A. MN 1st Inf. Co. A. Residence: Decorah, Winneshiek County, Iowa. Born 20 Aug. 1836 (Birth date on cemetery stone is "30 Aug.") near Oslo, Norway, son of Throne and Ingeborg (Terptad) Steen, who settled in Glenwood Township, east of Decorah. He was one of six Steen brothers to serve in the Civil War. Charles had been working in St. Paul before the war, working for Minnesota Governor Ramsey. Civil War: Age 26. Charles Steen enlisted for three years on 12 Apr. 1861, on the first day enlistments were accepted in Minnesota. Mustered as private at Fort Snelling, Minnesota, 29 Apr. 1861. Advanced to corporal, sergeant and then first sergeant. Took part in the battles of Bull Run, Virginia, July 1861; Marvin Hill, Fair Oaks and Seven Pines, Virginia; Antietam, Maryland, Sept. 1862; Fredericksburg, Virginia, Dec. 1862; Chancellorsville and Spotsylvania, Virginia, 1863; and Gettysburg, Pennsylvania. He was wounded in the Battle of Gettysburg, 2 July 1863, a minie ball through his left thigh. His leg was amputated in a hospital at Gettysburg. He was discharged from the service 3 May 1864. Postwar: Married Karen "Carrie" M. Paulson (17 Aug. 1843-23 Oct. 1925) on 21 Mar. 1867 at Decorah. Two children. He became Winneshiek County, Iowa, Recorder, serving from 1874 until 1877 when he died. His death was due to his war wound never having fully healed. Died 31 July 1877 at Decorah. Buried at Decorah Lutheran Cemetery. Sources: (MINN p.20) (MCIW p.51) (DGA) (ULVESTAD p.261) (Orlando C. Scholl, *History of the Steen Family,* 1964) (Edwin C. Bailey, *Past and Present of Winneshiek County, Iowa,* Vol. I, Chicago, 1913, p.312) (KJR).

STEEN, Henry IA 12th Inf. Co. G. Residence: Decorah, Winneshiek County, Iowa. Born 20 Sep. 1843 near Oslo, Norway, one of the six Civil War sons of Throne and Ingeborg (Terptad) Steen of Glenwood Township, east of Decorah, Iowa. Came to America in 1853. Civil War: Age 18. He enlisted for three years on 21 Oct. 1861. Mustered 5 Nov. 1861 at Dubuque, Iowa. Private. The 12th Iowa was part of the 15th and 16th Army Corps of the Army of Tennessee. Steen took part in battles for Fort Henry and Fort Donelson, Feb. 1862. Missing in battle of Shiloh, Tennessee, on 6 Apr. 1862 and captured by Rebel forces. He was sent to Libby prison in Richmond, Virginia. Paroled 28 May 1862. Was back with his company by 31 Aug. 1862. Took part in the siege of Vicksburg, Mississippi, July 1863, and the capture of Jackson, Mississippi, Aug. 1863. Reenlisted as a Veteran Volunteer 25 Dec. 1863 and re-mustered 5 Jan. 1864. Promoted to corporal 11 Feb. 1864. Fought in the battles of Nashville, Tennessee, 13-14 Dec. 1864; Spanish Fort, Alabama, 12 Apr. 1865; Fort Blakeley, Alabama, and the capture of Mobile, Alabama. Mustered out 20 Jan. 1866, at Memphis, Tennessee. Postwar: He married Inger Admundson (Chilson?) on 17 May 1866 at Decorah. Five children. Inger died 7 Jan. 1882. Henry became a merchant in Oakland, Nebraska. He married Emma Lucille Sprauge on 15 Sep. 1885 at Golden Spring, Nebraska. Two children. Later, he moved to Manassas, Virginia, where he worked as a guard at the Manassas National Battlefield Park. From there, he moved to the state of Washington. In 1925, he entered the Soldier's Home in Retsil, Washington. Died aged 94 on 21 Mar. 1938 at Retsil. Buried in Old Soldiers Cemetery at Retsil. Sources: (ISW-II p.531) (Orlando C. Scholl, *Steen Family History,* 1964) (DGA obituaries)

STEEN, John IA 12th Inf. Co. G. Residence: Decorah, Winneshiek County, Iowa. Born 20 Oct. 1841 near Oslo, Norway, one of the six Civil War sons of Throne and Ingeborg (Terptad) Steen of Glenwood Township, east of Decorah. Civil War: Age 20. Enlisted for three years on 21 Oct. 1861. Mustered 1 Nov. 1861 at Dubuque, Iowa. Private. Took part in the battles for Fort Henry and Fort Donelson, Tennessee, in Feb. 1862. Missing in action in the battle of Shiloh, Tennessee, 6 Apr. 1862. He had been captured and sent to Libby prison in Richmond, Virginia. Exchanged 31 Oct. 1862. Promoted to corporal 29 Apr. 1863. Took part in the siege of Vicksburg, Mississippi, July 1863. Reenlisted as a Veteran Volunteer on 31 Dec. 1863. Promoted to quartermaster sergeant 1 Jan. 1864. Fought in the battles of Tupelo, Mississippi, 13-15 July 1864; Spanish Fort, Alabama, 12 Apr. 1864; Fort Blakeley, Alabama, and the capture of Mobile, Alabama. Mustered out 20 Jan. 1866, at Memphis, Tennessee. Postwar: He married Marie Louise Hough on 10 Sep. 1870 at Decorah. Four children. Went to Omaha, Nebraska, after the war and worked as a mail clerk on an Omaha to Council Bluffs, Iowa, train. In 1877, he moved to Wahoo, Nebraska, and opened a hardware store with his brother, Otto. He became Postmaster of Wahoo in the early 1880s. After retiring from his Post Office career and his hardware business, he moved to Boise, Idaho. Died 23 Mar. 1923 at Wahoo. Buried at Sunrise Cemetery in Wahoo. Sources: (ISW-II p.531) (ULVESTAD p.261) (DGA) (Orlando C. Scholl, *Steen Family History,* 1964)

STEEN, Martin T. IA 38th Inf. Co. E. Residence: Decorah, Winneshiek County, Iowa. Born near Oslo, Norway, on 13 Feb. 1834. One of the six Civil War sons of Throne and Ingeborg (Terptad) Steen of Glenwood Township, east of Decorah, Iowa. Civil War: Age 28. Enlisted for three years on 14 Aug. 1862. Mustered 4 Nov. 1862 at Dubuque, Iowa. Private. Promoted to sergeant 1 July 1864. Transferred to Iowa 34th and 38th Infantry Consolidated, Company K, on 1 Jan. 1865. Fought in the siege of Vicksburg, Mississippi, in July 1863; and of Fort Morgan in 1864. He also was in the battles of Spanish Fort, Alabama; Fort Blakeley, Alabama; and in the capture of Mobile, Alabama, in Apr. 1865. Wounded at Fort Blakeley. Mustered out 15 Aug. 1865, at Houston, Texas. Postwar: He went to Buena Vista County, Iowa. Married Martha Marie Blilie, daughter of Peder and Marie Blilie, on 19 June 1871 at Buena Vista. Ten children. In 1875, he moved to Lake Mills, Iowa. Farmed until retiring in 1907. Died 16 Jan. 1918 in Frankville Township near Decorah, Iowa, of a stroke suffered four days earlier. Buried at Pontoppidan Lutheran Cemetery, Glenwood Township, near Decorah. Sources: (ISW-V p.486, 920) (Orlando C. Scholl, *Steen Family History*, 1964) (ULVESTAD p.261) (DGA obituary) "Stein, Martin"

STEEN, Otto F. WI 15th Inf. Co. K. Residence: Glenwood Township, Winneshiek County, Iowa. Born 21 Jan. 1846 near Oslo, Norway. Came to America in 1853 with his parents Throne and Ingeborg (Terptad) Steen who settled in Glenwood Township, east of Decorah, Iowa. There were eight Steen brothers and six of them were in the Union Army. Civil War: Unmarried. Enlisted for three years on his 16th birthday, 21 Jan. 1862 in Winneshiek County, and mustered at Madison, Wisconsin, 11 Feb. 1862. Private. Otto was his regiment's youngest man. He was promoted to corporal 1 July 1862. He was with the provisions transport from Stevenson, Alabama, in Oct. 1863. Was on recruiting duty in Dec. 1863. Took part in the battles of Perryville, Kentucky, Oct. 1862; Stones River, 31 Dec. 1862 and 1 Jan. 1863; Chickamauga, Sep. 1863; Missionary Ridge, 1863. Promoted to sergeant on 1 Apr. 1864. Wounded and taken prisoner in the battle at New Hope Church, Georgia, 27 May 1864. Was a prisoner in Andersonville, Georgia, for nine months. When he was liberated on 25 Feb. 1865, he was said to be very frail, little more than skin and bones. Mustered out at Madison, Wisconsin, 14 Apr. 1865. Postwar: He went to Wahoo, Nebraska, and operated a hardware store with his brother, John. He married Emma C. Hough Young on 22 July 1874 at Eldorado, Iowa. They had four children. Emma came into the marriage with a daughter from her first marriage. Otto died 3 Sept. 1930 at Boise, Idaho. Buried at Morris Hill Cemetery in Boise. Sources: (SHSW Series 1200, box 76-12; *Red Book*, vol. 20, p.140) (ULVESTAD p.261) (BUSLETT p.643, photo) (DGA) (AGER p.221, photo; p.319) (Orlando C. Scholl, *Steen Family History*, 1964) (ancestry.com)

STEEN, Theodore IA 12th Inf. Co. G. Residence: Decorah, Winneshiek County, Iowa. Born 20 Nov. 1838 near Oslo, Norway. Theodore was one of the six Civil War sons of Throne and Ingeborg (Terptad) Steen of Glenwood Township, east of Decorah, Iowa. Civil War: Age 23. Enlisted 21 Oct. 1861. Mustered 5 Nov. 1861 at Dubuque as a corporal. Took part in the capture of Fort Henry and Fort Donelson, Tennessee, in Feb. 1862. Missing in battle 6 Apr. 1862, Shiloh, Tennessee. He had been captured by Rebel forces and sent to Libby Prison, Richmond, Virginia. He was paroled 28 May 1862. Was released from parole on 31 Oct. 1862. Was back on the company rolls November 1862, listed as "absent sick." As of Jan. 1863, he was listed as present and on duty. Took part in the siege of Vicksburg, Mississippi; the capture of Jackson, Mississippi, Aug. 1863; and the campaign for Meridian, Mississippi, in Nov. 1863. Reenlisted as a Veteran Volunteer 25 Dec. 1863. Took part in the battle of Tupelo, Mississippi, 13-15 July 1864, and the battle of Nashville, Tennessee, 14-15 Dec. 1864. Was in the battle for Spanish Fort, Alabama, 12 Apr. 1865. Promoted to sergeant 1 Mar. 1865; mustered out 20 Jan. 1866, at Memphis, Tennessee. Postwar: Married Ellena Suckow on 28 May 1866 at Fort Dodge, Iowa. Two children. Lived in Buena Vista County, Iowa; then moved to Nebraska. Died 28 Sep. 1880 at Omaha, Nebraska. Buried in Greenwood Cemetery, Wahoo, Nebraska. Sources: (ISW-II p.531) (ULVESTAD p.261) (DGA) (Orlando C. Scholl, *Steen Family History*, 1964)

STEENSLAND, Ole WI 15th Inf. Co. E. Residence: Moscow, Iowa County, Wisconsin. Ole Steensland was born 29 Apr. 1842 at Steinsland farm in Hjelmeland, Rogaland, Norway, son of Erik Asbjornson, who was born 1799 in Aakre, Ullensvang, Hardanger, and his wife, Ingeborg Olsdatter, who was born 1809 at farm Borve in Ullensvang. They came to America in 1854. He was a brother of Asbjorn Steensland of WI 46th Inf. Co. F. Civil War: Age 19. Unmarried. Enlisted for three years on 28 Oct. 1861 in Iowa County. Mustered 8 Dec. 1861 at Madison, Wisconsin. Private. Missing in Battle of Chickamauga, Georgia, 20 Sept. 1863. Taken up from missing on 30 June 1864, when it was learned that he was a prisoner of war in Richmond, Virginia. He spent more than 19 months in Libby and Andersonville prisons. He was exchanged out of Andersonville on 1 Apr. 1865. Discharged 30 May 1865. Postwar: Died at Blanchardville, Wisconsin, on 15 Aug. 1902 and was buried at Perry, Daleyville, Wisconsin. Sources: (SHSW Series 1200, box 76-7; *Red Book*, vol. 20, p.78) (TAR) (BUSLETT p.493) (ULVESTAD p.330) (AGER p.166, photo; p.306) (GJERTVEIT) (Wisconsin Cemetery Records) (ancestry.com) (email from Bjarne Jormeland, Tananger, Norway, forwarded by Scott Cantwell Meeker) "Stensland, Ole"

TORKILDSON, Andrew WI 15th Inf. Co. A. Residence: Chicago, Illinois. Born "Andreas Torkilsen" at Bakke Parish in Lister and Mandal, Vest-Agder, Norway, about 1827. He was a son of Torkil Aanesen, a well-to-do farmer. Andreas had seven years of experience in the Swedish-Norwegian army. Came to America with his wife and children, settled in Chicago as a cooper. Civil War: Age 34. Married. On 27 Sept. 1861, he was authorized by Wisconsin Governor Randall to recruit a company of troops, which he soon did, becoming its captain. Appointed captain 11 Nov. 1861. Commissioned 12 Nov. 1861. Mustered 22 Dec. 1861 at Madison, Wisconsin. He tired of life at war and resigned 14 Oct. 1862. Postwar: Became a policeman in Chicago after the war; eventually went to Fort Dodge, Iowa, where he ran a cooper business. Sources: (SHSW Series 1200, box 76-3; *Red Book*, vol. 20, p.14) (BUSLETT p.338; LONN p.260) (AGER p.290) (ULVESTAD p.256) (GJERTVEIT) (MEEKER) (Odd S. Lovoll, *A Century of Urban Life*, Northfield: Norwegian-American Historical Association, 1988, p. 84) "Torkelsen, Andreas" "Torkilsen, Andrew" "Torkildsen, Andreas"

WILLIAMS, Augustus U.S. Navy. Born 1842 in Kristiansand, Norway. Civil War: Enlisted from Massachusetts. Seaman. Awarded the Medal of Honor. On board the *U.S.S. Santiago de Cuba* during the assault by the fleet on Fort Fisher, on 15 Jan. 1865. When the landing party to which he was attached charged on the fort with a cheer and with determination to plant their colors on the ramparts, Williams remained steadfast when they reached the foot of the fort and more than two-thirds of the marines and sailors fell back in panic. Taking cover when the enemy concentrated his fire on the remainder of the group, Williams alone remained with his executive officer, subsequently withdrawing from the field after dark. Sources: (*America's Medal of Honor Recipients*, 1977, pp.258, 1022)

WILLIAMS, Peter U.S. Navy. Born 1831 in Norway. Civil War: Enlisted from Pennsylvania. Awarded the Medal of Honor. As quartermaster on board the ironclad steamer *U.S.S. Monitor*, at Hampton Roads, at the mouth of the James River, on 9 Mar. 1862, he was at the helm. During the engagement between the *U.S.S. Monitor* and the *C.S.S. Merrimac*, the *Merrimac* was trying to attack the warship *Minnesota*, which was grounded on a sand bar and awaiting the next high tide. The *Monitor* went forth to protect the *Minnesota*. Williams "gallantly served throughout the engagement, piloting the *Monitor* throughout the battle which ended when the *Merrimac*, after being damaged, retired from the scene of the battle." When a shell from the *Merrimac* slammed into the pilot house and blinded Captain John Worden, Williams never left his post. Sources: (*America's Medal of Honor Recipients*, 1977, pp. 259, 1022) (*Medal of Honor Recipients 1863-1994*, vol. 1, Facts on File, Inc., 1995, p.243) (http://www.homeofheroes.com/moh/citations_1862)

WROLSTAD, John Olson WI 15th Inf. Co. I. Residence: New Hope, Portage County, Wisconsin. Born 8 Apr. 1839 in Turdal, Drangedal Parish, Norway, the son of Ole Olsen Wraalstad. Came to America in 1843 with his parents and lived the first year in the Muskego, Wisconsin, settlement. They lived for the next 12 years in the Rock River settlement; then came to New Hope, where they were living when the war began. Civil War: Age 21. Unmarried. Enlisted for three years on 5 Nov. 1861 at Scandinavia, Wisconsin, and mustered at Madison, Wisconsin, 20 Dec. 1861. Private. Appointed sergeant 1 Feb. 1862. Was with the provisions transport from Stevenson, Alabama, in Oct. 1863. Mustered out with I Company, 10 Feb. 1865, at Chattanooga, Tennessee. He was living in 1894 in Scandinavia, Wisconsin, where he ran a lumber business. Died in Northland, Wisconsin, on 13 Dec. 1907. Buried at New Hope Cemetery, Iola, Wisconsin. Sources: (SHSW Series 1200, box 76-11; *Red Book*, vol. 20, p.126) (BUSLETT p.612, photo) (AGER p.121, photo; p.316) (ULVESTAD pp.261-262) (Marwin Wrolstad, St. Paul, Minnesota.) (GJERTVEIT) (Wisconsin Cemetery Records) "Wraalstad, John" "Rolstad, John" "Roalstad, John Olsen"

Database Sources

AGER

Waldemar Ager, *Oberst Heg og hans Gutter,* Eau Claire: Fremad Publishing Co., 1916. (Photo page numbers are from this edition.) English translation is Waldemar Ager, *Colonel Heg and His Boys,* Northfield: Norwegian-American Historical Association, 2000. (Page numbers are from the Norwegian edition except those marked with the letter "e," which are from the translation.)

BLEGEN

Theodore C. Blegen, *Norwegian Migration to America,* Northfield: Norwegian-American Historical Association, 1940.

BUSLETT

O.A Buslett, *Det Femtende Regiment,* Decorah: B. Anundsen, 1894. *The Fifteenth Wisconsin by O.A. Buslett,* trans., Barbara C. Scott, 1999, available from State Historical Society of Wisconsin. (Page numbers are from the Norwegian edition except those marked with the letter "e," which are from the translation.)

DCHS

Douglas County, Minnesota, Historical Society.

FCHS

Freeborn County, Minnesota, Historical Society.

GJERTVEIT

Lars Gjertveit of Bodø, Norway, has made a listing of the Field Officers of the 15th Wisconsin Regiment Infantry.

GPO

"The Martyrs who, for our country, gave up their lives in the prison pens in Andersonville, GA," Quartermaster General's Office, 1866.

GRIMSRUD

Dee Anna Grimsrud is a reference archivist at the State Historical Society of Wisconsin in Madison, Wisconsin, and an authority on Wisconsin's Civil War soldiers, especially those of the 15th Regiment.

HEDBERG

Blaine Hedberg holds the Gerhard B. Naeseth Chair at Vesterheim Genealogical Center and Naeseth Library in Madison, Wisconsin.

HEG

The Civil War Letters of Hans Christian Heg, ed. Theodore C. Blegen, Northfield: Norwegian-American Historical Association, 1936.

ILSA

"Adjutant General Military and Naval Department Muster and Descriptive Rolls, 1861-1865," Illinois State Archives Microfilm.

ISW

Roster and Record of Iowa Soldiers in the War of the Rebeliion, Vols. 1-6, Des Moines: Iowa General Assembly Roster Board, 1908. Also available on a CD.

IVAL

Steve Meyer, *Iowa Valor,* Garrison Meyer Publishing, 1994.

JR

Jerry Rosholt, Vesterheim Norwegian-American Museum, Decorah, Iowa, visiting cemeteries.

LARSEN

Richard Larsen, Oregon, Wisconsin. Civil War researcher.

LARSON

Bruce Larson, Minneapolis, Minnesota. Civil War researcher.

LONN

Ella Lonn, *Foreigners in the Union Army and Navy*, Louisiana State University Press, 1951.

LOVE

William DeLoss Love, *Wisconsin in the War of the Rebellion*, Chicago: Church and Goodman, 1866. Pages 1056-1136 list the men from all Wisconsin units who were killed in action, died of wounds, or died of disease.

MCIW

Minnesota in the Civil and Indian Wars, 1861-1865, Legislature of Minnesota Act of 16 Apr. 1889, 1890.

MEEKER

Scott Campbell Meeker, "Roster of the 15th Wisconsin Volunteer Infantry Regiment" (compiled from *Roster of Wisconsin Volunteers, War of the Rebellion, 1861-1865*, published in 1886, and from other sources) posted on the Internet 29 Nov. 1998.

MINN

Annual Report of the Adjutant General of the State of Minnesota, Pioneer Printing Co., 1866.

MSAW

Franklin F. Holbrook, *Minnesota in the Spanish-American War*, St. Paul: Minnesota War Records Commission, 1923.

NELSON

History of the Scandinavians and Successful Scandinavians in the United States, Vols. I and II, Minneapolis: O. N. Nelson & Co., 1900.

ONI

Our Norwegian Immigrants, ed. John Thallaug and Rolf Erickson, Oslo: Dreyers Forlag, 1978.

OUDENSTAD

Halvard Oudenstad, *Utvandringen til Amerika*, Gjøvik Historical Society, 1981.

PENSION LIST

"The Executive Documents printed by order of the Senate of the United States for the second session of the 47th Congress, 1882-83," list of pensioners on the roll, 1 Jan. 1883.

QUINER

E. B. Quiner, *The Military History of Wisconsin in the War for the Union*, Chicago: Clarke & Co., 1866. Republished, Hudson: St. Croix Valley Civil War Round Table, 2000.

RYGG

A. N. Rygg, *Norwegians in New York 1825-1925*, Brooklyn: Norwegian News Company, 1941.

RUS

Janet Hewett, *The Roster of Union Soldiers 1861-1865*, Wilmington: Broadfoot Publishing Co., 1998.

RW

Roster of Wisconsin Volunteers, War of the Rebellion, 1861-1865, Vols. I and II, compiled under direction of the Adjutant General, Madison: 1886.

SDSHS WPA

Veterans' Cemetery Gravesites. South Dakota State Historical Society, Pierre, South Dakota.

SHSW

State Historical Society of Wisconsin, Madison, Wisconsin, 259 boxes.

Series 1200: Records of Civil War Regiments, 1861-1900, records of the Wisconsin Adjutant General's Office.

Red Book, popular name for *Series 1144 Regimental and Descriptive Rolls,* a series of books, one for each military unit, containing information copied in 1866 from the *Series 1200* records.

Blue Book, similar to the *Red Book,* but copied 25 years later, also from the *Series 1200* records. These came about to aid veterans in applying for pensions. They include more information relating to battles in which a soldier served.

TAR

Payroll muster rolls of Wisconsin 15th Company E, saved by Captain T. A. Rossing. Held by Luther College Library, Decorah, Iowa.

ULVESTAD

Martin Ulvestad, *Nordmændene I Amerika,* Minneapolis: History Book Co., 1907.

WALK

Violet Walk, Grafton, Iowa. Mrs. Walk is completing a survey of all Worth County, Iowa, residents who served in the Civil War and of all Civil War veterans who later lived in Worth County.

WLCW

Charles Edward Esterbrook, *Wisconsin Losses in the Civil War,* published by state printer, Madison, Wisconsin, 1915.

XSS

William L. Alexander, *List of Ex-Soldiers, Sailors and Marines, Living in Iowa,* Des Moines: 1886.

Note: Some individuals are listed as sources in the database by name only. Contact information for these individuals is available through Vesterheim.

Where to Look

Books About Norwegian Soldiers

Waldemar Ager, an editor in Eau Claire, Wisconsin, in 1916 wrote *Oberst Heg og hans Gutter*. This book was translated and published in 2000 by the Norwegian-American Historical Association, Northfield, Minnesota, under the title *Colonel Heg and his Boys*.

Theodore C. Blegen, Dean of the Graduate School in the University of Minnesota, wrote a two volume work called *Norwegian Migration to America*, published in 1940 by the Norwegian-American Historical Association, Northfield, Minnesota.

O. A. Buslett (Ole Amundsen Buslett) of Stevens Point, Wisconsin, wrote *Det Femtende Regiment* in 1894, the story of Wisconsin's famous all-Norwegian 15th Regiment. He included many anecdotes and letters. This book was translated in 1999 by Barbara G. Scott of Ripon, Wisconsin, and copies are available from Dee Grimsrud at the State Historical Society of Wisconsin Archives.

Edwin B. Quiner, a journalist and printer in Madison, began gathering Wisconsin stories early in the war, and by late 1863 had begun work on a history of Wisconsin regiments. His *Military History of Wisconsin* was published in 1866. Quiner died two years later, at age 52. His book was republished in 2000 by the St. Croix Valley Civil War Round Table of Hudson, Wisconsin.

William DeLoss Love, a Milwaukee clergyman, prepared a history similar to that of Quiner's. It was called *Wisconsin in the War of the Rebellion* and was published also in 1866. The book is almost impossible to find. The Archives section of the State Historical Society of Wisconsin has a copy.

Martin Ulvestad (Ole Johannes Martinus Ulvestad) wrote a huge book called *Nordmændene I Amerika*, published in 1906 and 1913, which includes a section on Civil War soldiers. He has many duplicate entries. Since the American military tended to identify Norwegian enlistees as "born in Sweden," Ulvestad is the place to look to identify which of these is really Norwegian.

Other Sources

Obituaries

Obituaries gathered by county historical societies; privately printed family histories (the Vesterheim Genealogical Center and Naeseth Library in Madison, Wisconsin, has many); and hundreds of internet web sites.

Military Records

Soldiers were to be paid every other month (and sometimes were) and company clerks prepared muster rolls listing all members of the company and showing which soldiers were on hand to get their money. Each of these muster rolls was copied from the one used two months earlier, and each showed the soldier's name, place of birth, age, enlistment dates and rank. Each company clerk kept one copy, sent one to the regimental headquarters, sent one to the War Department in Washington, D.C., and one to the adjutant general of the state from which the unit came. At the close of the war, legislatures ordered that this information be copied into books and that was done. In some states – Wisconsin is one – the original muster rolls still exist.

Websites

Vesterheim Norwegian-American Museum's website includes an extensive listing of Norwegian immigrants in American wars. The listing is updated periodically with the results of ongoing research.

www.vesterheim.org

The roster of the Wisconsin 15th Volunteer Infantry regiment is available on a site constructed by Scott Cantwell Meeker. The site includes many photos and individual stories of the men of the Wisconsin 15th.

www.15thwisconsin.com

Photo Credits

Page 2/3: 1880 Regimental Reunion of the Wisconsin 15th
Andreas Larsen Dahl, photographer
Wisconsin Historical Society, image WHi 5259

Page 4: (Detail) Lieutenant Ole A. Anderson, Iowa 3rd Infantry,
Company D
Vesterheim Norwegian-American Museum Archive

Those Steen Boys:

Page 12: Thrond and Ingeborg Steen
Vesterheim Norwegian-American Museum Archive, Steen Collection
(Other photos, see below.)

Page 14: Sergeant Charles A. Steen, Minnesota 1st Infantry,
Company A
Vesterheim Norwegian-American Museum Archive, Steen Collection

Page 16: Sergeant Otto Steen, Wisconsin 15th Infantry, Company K
Vesterheim Norwegian-American Museum Archive, Steen Collection

Page 17: Corporal Henry Steen, Iowa 12th Infantry, Company G
Sergeant John Steen, Iowa 12th Infantry, Company G
Vesterheim Norwegian-American Museum Archive, Steen Collection

Page 18: Sergeant Martin Steen, Iowa 38th Infantry, Company E
Vesterheim Norwegian-American Museum Archive, Steen Collection

A Thousand Oles:

Page 20: Brevet Captain Ole K. Hanson, Wisconsin 15th Infantry,
Company A
Wisconsin Historical Society, image WHi 5260

Peace. Pox. Potatoes.

Page 22/23: Thorhaugen, a farm in Gol, Hallingdal
Photo by E.T. Braaten
Vesterheim Norwegian-American Museum Archive, Thea Sando
Collection, gift of Isabelle Larson

Page 24: Farm in Hallingdal
Vesterheim Norwegian-American Museum Archive, Thea Sando
Collection, gift of Isabelle Larson

And They Were Heroes:

Page 28/29: Crewmen on the deck of the *Monitor*
Naval Historical Center, image NH 574

Page 31: (Detail) Pilot Peter Williams
Naval Historical Center, image NH 574

Page 32: Line engraving of the *Monitor*, 1862
Naval Historical Center, image NH 76324-KN

15th Wisconsin:

Page 34: The Nora Society banner
Vesterheim Norwegian-American Museum, object LC 900, Luther
College Collection

Page 35: The reverse side of Nora Society banner, features 34 stars,
the number of states in the Union in 1861.
Vesterheim Norwegian-American Museum, object LC 900, Luther
College Collection

Men of the 15th

To Each His Story:

Civil War Digest: